STORIES AND ESSAYS

Swallowing the
Golden Stone

Walter Wangerin, Jr.

To Maurice Sendak

with admiration and gratitude
this collection is dedicated,
for his has been the truest eye
into the loamy soil of childhood,
dark and deep and rich and blooming after all

SWALLOWING THE GOLDEN STONE
Stories and Essays

Published in association with the literary agency of Alive Communications, 1465 Kelly Johnson Blvd., Suite 320, Colorado Springs, CO 80920.

Large-quantity purchases or custom editions of this book are available at a discount from the publisher. For more information, contact the sales department at Augsburg Fortress, Publishers, 1-800-328-4648, or write to: Sales Director, Augsburg Fortress, Publishers, P.O. Box 1209, Minneapolis, MN 55440-1209.

Library of Congress Cataloging-in-Publication Data
Wangerin, Walter.
    Swallowing the golden stone : stories and essays / by Walter Wangerin, Jr.
        p. cm.
    Summary: A collection of stories, essays, and poems, including "Lowercase People," "Elisabeth and the Water-Troll," and "To Weave a World."
    ISBN 0-8066-3710-2 (alk. paper)
    1. Children's literature. [1. Literature—Collections.] I. Title.
PZ7.W1814 Sw2001   2001033641

Cover design by Marti Naughton
Book design by Michelle L. N. Cook

The paper used in this publication meets the minimum requirements of American National Standard for Information Sciences—Permanence of Paper for Printed Library Materials, ANSI Z329.48-1984. ⊖ ™

Printed in Canada   AF 9-3710

05   04   03   02   01   1   2   3   4   5   6   7   8   9   10

Contents

Lowercase People

 with his belly, but sits and looks. What can an old man see?

 comes into my room.

 pinches him.

 turns 'round and marches out of the room again.

 eats corn on the cob.

 can't; she has buck teeth.

 hangs one leg over her seat.

 has the answer: "Teacher, teacher, call on me!"

i can hide, the littlest soldier of all; that's me.

in the day, is a cheerleader, jumping;
at night she kneels to pray.

 can't see; he walks with a white cane tapping.

 might sneeze.

 says things like, "The bees's
knees," then tickles me with
kisses—because  is the moustache
on my daddy's lip.

 all alone,
is waiting
for someone
to choose her,
too.

holds his nose high in the air.

has a big mouth:
"Off!" he hollers.
"Get off my bike!"

 and play chequers together.

who just threw a rock,
is scared it'll break the window.

 is deceitful,
smiling one way and frowning the other.

 takes big bites.

 has his nose to the ground
and his legs stuck up in the air.

 "Hooray!"  dives down like a
hawk from the sky.

 is the face of my calico cat.

 is my cat's tail   and   is the face of the man my calico scratched,
the face of the fellow whose window cracked,
the face of my brother whose bicycle crashed. . . .
Mad, mad, the angry s,
mad at the world and me!

While I and my daddy eat corn on the cob
with , whom I chose as my friend;

 , , and sing, "Hip, hooray!"
since and have come to play

with , ,

So *that's* what the man with the belly can see:
a party of letters—plus , that's me—
an abecedarian fiddle-dee-dee,
an alphabet of friends.

, and .

Foreword

Children have the capacity to animate any inanimate thing. They give face and character to the clouds. They hold earnest conversations with stones and fish and teddy bears. Wallpaper can make them giggle endlessly. A bug on the tip of a finger waves her feelers in solitary sorrow because her house is on fire and her children are gone. And all this is their lively, immediate response to the world: nothing is less alive than they are themselves.

When our son Joseph was two years old, he cried, "Look!" kneeling in the back of our traveling car, pointing out the window: "Look! The sun is following us in an Indian boat!" I looked. The sun, behind us, was half hidden by a long white cloud which, yes, was shaped exactly like a canoe.

When he was five and six and punished for some misdeed—told by his mother to "sit in the corner till you've decided to behave"—we marveled at how long and how patiently the child could endure the discipline. Then one day, while rearranging the living room furniture, we noticed that the walls were strangely dark behind the chairs, as if their shadows—precisely the shape of the chairs—had stayed stuck to the wall. Closer inspection, a most careful inspection, revealed that Joseph had pencil-drawn ten thousand, thousand tiny faces around every chip, dot, crack, and ripple on the wall.

The child's lively, *immediate* response to the world: in these cases no adult intervenes between children and the objects of their attention, the stuff quickened by their imaginations.

But when the time comes that we can and should intervene, to direct their fantasies, to teach them and lead them, to train up their souls in the ways they should go; but yet when we want neither to destroy these swift imaginations nor to break their lively relationship with the world around them, what is the best tool we have at hand?

Why, words.

Language.

And, thereby, stories.

We parents, grandparents, teachers, every adult who loves children and who has their ears have the remarkable opportunity (and, I believe, the generational responsibility) to present the stuff of *our* worlds (moral, cultural, scientific, spiritual, historical, humorous) to their imaginations *also* for rich relationships. But that "stuff," as well as the relationship that draws their rapt attentions, causing them in wonder to follow, is mediated by words. And pictures. Stories.

So I have begun this book of stories and essays with a simple demonstration of the child/world/adult nexus, "Lowercase People."

To Joseph, sun and cloud became an Indian who paddled the blue sky above at the same speeds with which we traveled the road below. Likewise, children may find faces and character in the letters of the alphabet—in the alphabetical figure itself, which otherwise is meant to symbolize some particular *sound.*

What we don't say is "Don't," as if they've gotten it wrong. As if the objective, analytic mind must murder the subjective, imagining one. Analysis permits one thing to be one thing only. It cancels fancy. Imagination, on the other hand, can refract one thing into a thousand (even contradictory) things, believing sweetly in all of them at once. It enriches analysis.

So what we do say is, "Do," and, "Here's how." We join the game. We learn and then we obey their natural, unexamined rules for the game; but then we, within the scope of that game, lead—with laughter and emotion and our palpable love, but especially with that which makes all these things manifest unto the child—with our talk.

> *While I and my daddy eat corn on the cob*
> *with L, whom I chose as my friend . . .*

See? Language, leading the fancy, may assure the child of a strong, protective companionship (the "daddy" whose moustache tickles with kisses), even while it advises the child likewise to companion others, the lonely, the *L* all alone, who was waiting for someone to choose her, too.

I am a writer. This is my profession. Among all the other literary genres I've produced over the years is this: that I tell, write, and publish stories for children. I have, therefore, given a great deal of thought to this consequential thing which the generations accomplish together, telling and hearing stories, spinning the yarn and wearing it, too.

This book contains a number of my children's stories (some of which have been published independently as picture books, while others are new and heretofore unpublished). This book also gives me the opportunity to comment both upon individual stories and upon the practice as a whole. I'll make my comments as a professional, probing the mechanics and the effects of my profession. But I'll make them personal as well, drawing freely from any corner of my interest or character or convictions (which must include not only my craft, my intent and intellect and purposes, but also my spirit and my faith, for no author writes *divorced* from the premises and the axioms whereby he or she interprets the universe). And I will direct these comments especially to the adults, to those of you who also are interested in this practice, whether you tell, teach, or teach the telling of children's stories.

Look, then, for personal comments to follow each of the stories collected here.

And find, too, longer discursive essays as we go along.

On the other hand, I don't intend to *interpret* the narrative material. That task belongs to others, readers and critics, as an author's interpretive analysis of his writing ("What is your message? What are you trying to say?") can only narrow and straighten the more evocative thing: art which as art invites countless responses. It is as various and as living as the variety and the lives of those who experience it. But art bound to a single interpretation is confined to a single propositional "theme": as cold on the table as an eyeless fish.

Elisabeth and the Water-Troll

Prologue: The Well, the Troll, Elisabeth

 n ancient path goes north from the village of Dorf. It cuts through the fields and the woods, drops down into a valley, then winds across the valley floor till it ends at a well. The villagers know this well. They call it "Despair."

It's an old, old well—older than any remember; and cold because the shaft goes deep, deep into the earth; and still. Its stones are green, all covered with moss. Lizards slip between the cracks. Lizards peep out with leatherlike stares and vanish when the wind grows sharp—for the wind grows sharp indeed. It screams down the length of the valley, and *Hoooo!* it blows on the hole of the well. *Hoooo! Hoooo!*—which to the villager's ears sounds like, *You! You! I'll swallow you! I'll drink you like water and eat you like foooood!*

Nobody comes to the well. Or nobody nearly. The women who wash with water don't come, nor the men who drink cool water in the heat of the day, nor the children who play. Not even the dogs of the village will creep by the Well Despair, because they know. Everyone knows. For seven generations they've whispered the stories by firelight, shuddering, shivering, grave; and they know that deep in that well there dwells a Troll.

Ah, there it is. Now we have spoken it: the Troll! It's the *Troll* that parents use to scare their children indoors at night: "Come! Come! Or the Troll will get you. He'll drink you like water! He'll eat you like food!"

It's the *Troll* that causes the children to whimper while they are sleeping, dreaming, dreaming.

It's because of the *Troll* that grandparents and great-grandparents and great-*great*-grandparents named the well "Despair."

And every time his story is told, the Troll grows greener and grimmer and uglier.

Yes, the Troll. But what shall we *say* of him? What is the truth and not a story?

Well, he isn't a mole, because he's too much like a man. He frowns like a man. But he can't be a man exactly, either, because he digs in the darkness and shrinks from the light. Light hurts him as bad as fire can; but his hearing is as good as miracles. His arms are long and powerful. He has claws on his fingers and fangs in his mouth and green in his eyes, which glow; his green eyes glow in the dark. He leaps as lightly as a cat from ledge to ledge inside his well. His fur is thick; his back is bunched; his whiskers are wet—and always his brow is frowning because always he's trying to think, and thinking is hard for the Troll, who isn't a man exactly.

Nobody comes to the well. Or nobody nearly . . .

One day, suddenly, a small girl *does* appear in the terrible circle of daylight at the top of the well. She's shaking her head. She's sobbing: "Ow-ooo! Ow-ooooo!"

The Troll cannot look up without burning his eyes; but he listens, for the child is wailing like the wind, but she's younger and sadder than the wind, and the Troll hears the difference.

"Oh, Mama!" she wails. Like rain her tears spill down upon the Troll, but they are warmer than the rain; they sting like sorrow, and the Troll can feel the difference.

"Mama, why did you have to die?"

To die? The Troll covers his mouth and makes no sound.

"You lied to me," the child cries. "You said you loved me—but how can you love me and go away, too?" The Troll hears little fists hitting the stones above. "You didn't love Elisabeth. You died. You left me. Mama, Mama, you lied to me!"

Now the Troll hears the whip and crackle of the little girl's hair as she yanks something from it. Two somethings. "What do I want with your things?" she cries. "*Papa* wants me to wear your combs. Papa wants me to be glad again. But I don't *want* to be glad. And I don't *want* your combs. No! No!"

Something lands on the Troll's head. Two somethings—and they catch in his hair. He reaches and pulls out two tortoiseshell combs, in which he can smell love—the love of a mother, the love of a father—and the grief of a little girl, who is sobbing against the stones above, murmuring, "Gone, gone, gone, gone. No, I won't trust anyone, because everyone lies, lies, lies."

So speaks Elisabeth.

And now the Troll is frowning dreadfully. With green-glowing eyes, he's staring at two combs in his claws, and his heart is beating sorrow for the child above, and his nose—yes, and all his breathing—is filled with the love of the combs, and his forehead is frowning because he is trying to think one good and helpful thought.

Part One: To Dorf before the Dawn

here's a mist in the valley in moonlight. The sun will arise and burn that mist away. But first, while the people are sleeping, something darker and greener is arising.

The Troll is coming up.

His head and his shoulders heave over the well-stones. His eyes shine green in the night. His cat feet leap the mossy rock and with a loping gallop the Troll is running, running.

Across the valley floor, up the hills like a stallion he goes.

Over the fields, down empty roads, through woods, through gardens and gates—until he comes to the village of Dorf, where the houses are shut and the children are dreaming.

He stands by the church in the village square. Three times he turns around, sniffing the breezes, seeking the scent. Suddenly he sees grey light in the eastern sky: the dawn is coming, and he has to hurry.

Hurry, Troll!

> ONE, *he's the shadow that falls on the door.*
> TWO, *he's a cough in the night.*
> THREE, *he is counting the houses, till* FOUR,
> *He rears like a horse at the scent of a war—*
> THERE! *There is the house he is searching for:*
> *Small and wood and white.*

Softly the Troll creeps across the lawn. He puts his face to the window glass. He peers in with old, old eyes and sighs for what he sees.

"Bonnie Lass," he growls.

Inside the room on a little pillow lies Elisabeth asleep. She is so beautiful.

The Troll can move like water: anywhere, through any crack or crevice. Like water, then, he steals into her bedroom and holds his breath and bends over the child. His heart is rushing as hard as a river.

> *Elisabeth has pale white skin.*
> *The Troll is lifting her.*
> *Her hair so black, her arms so thin*

Hang like a broken violin.
The Troll begins to purr:

"Thee be . . ." he says. He swallows, unused to speaking, unused to so much feeling. "Beth, Beth," he says, "come be my little guest."

But quick! The dawn is coming!

Hurry, Troll. Begone before the sun.

Swiftly the Troll flies from the room with the child against his breast. Running, running, faster than sunrise, his long hair streaming, his breathing a wind in his chest—but tenderly he holds the child who sleeps and sleeps unknowing.

In the woods he leaps and sweeps through the trees like an owl in muffled flight.

Then down to the valley with galloping steps, and at the well he springs. He sails through the air and dives into his hole and in the blink of an eye he is gone.

When the sun arises that day, the valley is as empty as ever before. The Troll is deep underground, gazing upon the child Elisabeth. He has laid her in a lizard shell and spread her hair like a cloud around her. With a rough knuckle he brushes her cheek. And here is a wonder they never tell by firelight: he is weeping. The Troll is weeping to see this child so light on a ledge in the Well Despair, for her mouth is so sad, and her brow is so beautiful.

"Babe," he growls. "O baby best."

But he's frowning and frowning on account of a difficult thought: how to make one sad heart happy.

"Pretty, pretty, prettiest."

Part Two: Dorf in the Morning

ost of the village is still asleep, though the sun is rising, burning the mist away. Most of the people are dreaming dreams—but not for long.

One man is awake in Dorf, standing in the village square, wearing nothing but a nightshirt.

"Eliza?" he calls.

His hair is tangled. He hadn't the comb or the time to comb it. He turns 'round and 'round, peering into the shadows and crying, "Eliza?" louder and louder.

"Eliza Beth! Where are you?"

No one answers.

The poor man lifts two small slippers high in the air. "People!" he shouts. "People of Dorf! Friends and neighbors, has anyone seen my daughter? Does anyone know where Elisabeth's at?"

No one answers.

So the man runs to the church and enters it. He isn't young or strong or even straight. His back is hunched. But he knows how to pull a bell cord:

BONG!

The church bell has a deep round throat and a tongue of iron in order to cry out "Fire" or "Danger!" or "Death."

BONG!

Who can sleep when the bell is tolling? Windows fly open. Heads pop out, and the people say, "What's wrong? What's—"

BONG!

The Mayor stumbles from his doorway, yanking his belt above his belly. "Who?—"

BONG!

The Sheriff rushes down the street, strapping a sword to his side. "Where?—"

BONG!

Men grab clubs. Women run to the village square. "When?—"

BONG!

"Why?—"

BONG!

"Who's tolling that terrible bell?"

It's the Parson, finally, who goes to the church and stands outside the door and thunders: "That's it! That's it! Be ye flesh or be ye Devil, come out and show yourself! Come!"

The bell falls silent.

The Sheriff draws his sword. The men grip their clubs. The Mayor wishes he weren't the Mayor. . . .

But when the church door opens, no one but a bent-backed man comes out, wearing a nightshirt and pressing something muddy to his chest.

"Why, Peter! It's only Peter!" the Parson cries, and everyone grows a little bit bolder.

Then everyone grunts and gets angry.

The Sheriff slams his sword back into the scabbard. "You ought to be flogged," he gripes, "for destroying our sleep."

And the Mayor is glad to be Mayor again, the official voice of the village. He hitches his belt and clears his throat. "You'd better have good reason, sir, for ringing that bell," he says.

Peter whispers, "I do."

"Out with it," the Mayor commands, turning to face his citizens. "Tell us at once."

"Elisabeth," Peter whispers. "Elisabeth," he says and begins to sob.

"Yes? Yes?" the Mayor repeats. "Elisabeth—and *what?*"

"She's gone," Peter says.

"What? Your daughter is what? Speak up, man, so the people can hear you."

Peter throws back his head and howls, now, at the top of his lungs: "Elisabeth has been kidnapped!"

Immediately the people grow a little less bold. They all have children of their own. "Kidnapped?"

The Mayor sees fear in the people. "Well," he says. He hitches his belt up and shouts, "Well you're probably wrong. Yes, that's it: you're wrong, sir. Elisabeth just ran away."

"No!" Peter cries. "She *was* kidnapped. And it's worse than that. Look what I found in her bedroom." He lifts up what he was pressing against his chest: two small slippers, both of them muddy with a dark green slime.

"Little girls don't run away barefoot," Peter says. "And there's mud all over her bedroom, mud on her bed, mud on her windowsill. Something dripping and ugly has stolen my daughter away. Friends and neighbors, please, please help me find my daughter!"

Now the Mayor is wishing he weren't the Mayor again. He tries to talk, but can only squeak.

The people are deathly quiet, too, staring at the dark green slime.

Peter says softly, "Will you help me?"

But "Parson?" the people say. "Parson, what makes green slime?"

In his magnificent voice the Parson announces: "Well. I just. Hum. Don't know."

The worst is not to know.

Peter pleads, "Won't somebody help me?"

"Parson? Parson? But will the slimy one come back tonight?"

The Parson says, "Well . . ."

The people cry, "You mean he *might?*"

The Parson says, "Well . . ."

The people scream, "You mean he *will?*"

Now no one is bold any more. Everyone's scared. "He *will!*" the whole crowd shouts. "And whose is the next child he will steal?"

The Mayor has gone to his office to think. But soon another voice is booming above the crowd with force and authority.

"Follow me! Follow me!"

It's the Sheriff, his sword already drawn. "I'm a man of action! I know what to do!"

Oh, thank God for men of action. Thank God for something to do.

"Follow me, and we'll catch this muddy baby-snatcher and give him what he deserves. Evil given, evil gotten, right?"

This is the way the Sheriff thinks: tat for tit and tit for tat. Laws, laws run in his blood, and the men are glad and agree: "Right!"

"A slasher," booms the Sheriff, "should be slashed, right?"

This is the way the Sheriff thinks, bad to worse and worse to worst, and the men agree: "Right!"

"And a killer," the Sheriff roars, "should be killed, right?"

And all the men, exploding with boldness, cry, "Right!"

Soon there's no one left in the village square save one man in a nightshirt, hugging two small slippers and talking to himself.

"Eliza, you're barefoot," he says. To him this is an enormous sadness. "You're going to catch a cold," he says.

Suddenly he raises a hand to touch his tangled hair. "And yesterday you came home without your mother's combs! How could they have fallen from your beautiful hair?"

What an odd question to ask at this time. But the poor man asks it anyway: "Eliza, where are your tortoiseshell combs?"—because he cannot bear to ask the other question which has no answer:

Eliza, where are you?

Part Three: The Well in the Afternoon

All day long the child has been sleeping, the sad Elisabeth. But day is like night in the Well Despair. It is always dark down there.

And all day long the Troll has been busy—busier and happier than he has ever been before. In and out of his chambers, up and down his tunnels he's gone, arranging, preparing for the moment when the child will wake.

It broke his heart to feel her tears and to know how sad a girl can be. Therefore—

The Troll has made Elisabeth
A gown of grass, a glove of glass,
  A shawl of baby's breath.
He's shod her feet in shucks of wheat;
He's brought her buttercups to eat;
He's carved a diamond for her seat—

And when at last she stirs, when the little girl coughs and wakes and looks around, there! There is the Troll, smiling horribly.

"Ah, when she wakes," he saith,
"Thee be my Queenling, Beth."

That's what the Troll says through his fangs. And he means it kindly. But to the ears of a child it sounds savage, like an animal snarling.

Elisabeth is in the home of the Troll. He considers it a comfortable place. But to her eyes it's a dungeon where water drips all around. It's dark and cold, and lizards are twitching past her feet. She whimpers and starts to sit up.

Then a great monster with green-bright eyes begins to reach toward her, growling, "Bonnie Lass, someone cares for thee. And someone does not lie."

Long arms! Strong arms! Claws at the ends of his fingers! When one of these touches her face, Elisabeth jumps to her feet, screaming.

"Nay," growls the Troll, frowning frightfully. "Nay, I mean thee no harm—"

But it's harm Elisabeth hears. She starts to stumble backward.

"Stop!" the beast roars, and the caverns echo the word, and the poor girl turns and breaks into a run.

"Danger!" the beast bellows. "'Tis only a ledge in front of thee—"

One moment the child is running on stone, and the next she's sailing through empty air. "Papa!" she shrieks. "Papa! Papa!"

She somersaults backward. Above her she sees a circle of sky, below her a pit of perfect blackness. And now she's falling down—down and down the shaft of the Well Despair.

"Papaaaaaa!"

The Troll's not frowning any more, not thinking at all. There's no time to think. He's acting. He dashes to the edge of the ledge and leaps.

Elisabeth in a nightgown, her long hair streaming upward like a flag, sinks lightly. But the Troll has rolled himself into a ball and drops like a stone, fast and faster. Soon he passes her by. Then far below he flings out an arm and grabs at the wall. He finds a grip. He lurches to a stop, his body slamming against the rock; but with that one arm he hangs on, and with the other he sweeps the air and catches the falling child in the crook of the arm and saves her.

"Ohhh!" he cries. Their double weight has broken him. But he keeps the girl. He presses her against his ribs, and Elisabeth does the same: she winds her fingers in his hair and clings like an infant.

She is shivering.

For his own pain, the Troll groans wretchedly; but for her shivers he sings a soft lullaby: "Hush babe. Hush thee, baby best. I vow we'll climb it, and I'll lay thee on the solid ground again."

And here is a wondrous, blessed thing: Elisabeth understands him, and she believes him.

Slowly, slowly he starts to climb.

Elisabeth feels the hurtful flexing and hears his moan with every move. To her this is no longer an animal sound. It's deeper than that and kinder, too—as though she were hearing a holy river running in the regions of his heart.

Little Elisabeth ceases to shiver. Before they have ascended to the ledge, she trusts the strength and the promise of the Troll. She isn't cold. She's melting. She presses her cheek against his breast and begins to feel his hurt as if it were her own.

"Who are you?" the child whispers.

Slowly, slowly he gains the ledge again. Gently he lays her in the lizard shell. And then, his vow fulfilled, the Troll collapses beside her and does not move.

"Who are you?" Elisabeth whispers. "I don't even know your name."

But his eyelids are closed, the green lights covered, and he doesn't answer. All is silent.

No, not silent exactly. Water is dripping. Water runs in the deeps of his home. The sounds of water come from everywhere.

All at once the monster who lies before her draws a terrible breath and groans, and that too sounds like the flow of a mighty river—

Ahhh! Soon in her soul the child is remembering stories she heard by firelight. This is . . . this is the Troll, the *Water*-Troll! But the stories are wrong! The stories are wrong. He hasn't drunk her like water. He hasn't chewed her like food. He's caught her and saved her and suffered such pain for her. And the Water-Troll has leaked like kindness into her heart, has washed her anger away and given her pity instead. Of *course* water drips all around them now. This well is the source of the water of Dorf—and this one is the Water-Troll.

Elisabeth leans over him and starts to cry. She's crying because of his kindness and his pain—the first such tears she's wept since her mother died.

One by one the tears drop on the Water-Troll. They startle him. His green eyes open and glow upon her.

"What, child?" he growls. He raises a claw. "Art thou crying still? But I wanted to dry thy tears. Oh, pretty Beth," he sighs. "I did not want thee sad. I wanted to tell thee, life is lovelier than bad, and one somebody loves thee. One somebody does not lie."

The great Troll closes his eyes again. "But what hath my labors done for thee? Nothing but to frighten thee, and what is the good of that? Forgive this Troll. He should never have brought thee into his hole."

But the little Queenling cannot blame him. Instead, she smiles. Through the rain of her tears her smile is as bright as laughter and love. And that which happens next in the well is known by none for the telling by firelight.

> *"Oh, Troll," she says; and on his chest*
> *She lays her head as if to rest.*
> *Indeed, he is the ugliest,*
> *   But he needs comforting.*
> *So Beth begins to sing.*
>
> *For him she sings, "Alack-a-day."*
> *For him a pretty roundelay*
> *   To take the pain away:*
> *"Alas, and lack the day. . . ."*

Part Four: The Village in the Evening

he day is done, and the Sheriff is angry. He sits in the tavern glaring at his pint of ale and curses the day that produced no muddy green beast to slice with his sword.

The men of Dorf are also there, drinking pints in a gloomy silence. All day long they've followed the Sheriff, who followed the tracks of slime as far as the woods, peering down at the ground, finding not another green drop anywhere, failing, failing.

Parson? What makes green slime?

Well, I don't know.

The worst is not to know.

But the night is coming. The chill and the dark and the fear are coming. And dreams that no one wants to dream.

And what will come to steal the children? And whose child next will be taken tonight?

Mothers have bolted their doors. They've seen the mud on Elisabeth's sheets, signs of the evil in Peter's house—which, surely, they didn't want in theirs.

The Mayor is soaking his feet in a tub of water, trying to soothe his nerves.

The Parson is crouched in the baptistry, praying.

And Peter himself is washing those sheets, which terrified Dorfers everywhere. Slowly, slowly he wrings the white cloth: and sadly, sadly, for it seems he is washing his daughter away.

So the twilight dies. So the night comes down. So Peter looks up and out his window, and finally he asks the question he could not ask before:

"Liza? Liza Beth, where are you now?"

All at once, through the whole village of Dorf, a wonderful sound is heard from a wonderful source. The sound is singing! And the source is water—all of the water in Dorf!

Thirty-two mugs on the tavern tables break into song. One is the Sheriff's. He shatters it with his sword, while the rest of the men jump backward, astonished.

The Mayor's tub begins to sing. He yelps and falls and spills it everywhere.

The village pump joins in.

The water in the baptistry sings soprano.

Puddles and runnels, brooks and ponds, cups and kettles and pots: a thousand voices are singing one song:

Alas, they sing. *Alas, alack-a-day!*

All of Dorf is a choir now, and all of its people are terrified. All but one.

Little, bent-backed Peter is listening to the water that washes the sheets, and he's grinning! He's clapping his hands. And he's laughing.

This is the song he taught his daughter to sing! This is Elisabeth's voice, *Alas, alack-a-day.*

But the voice is lovelier, older somehow. And she's singing new verses about a well, a shell, a glove of glass, and a wounded creature whom she loves, whose name is, whose name is—

⁂

"I know! I know!" Peter shouts in the middle of the village square. "I know where Elisabeth's at!"

"What?" The first one to come is the Sheriff, mad and getting madder. "Where?" he demands.

"Yes," laughs Peter, "and I know who has her, too!"

Here come the men with their clubs, lighting torches, yelling, "Who? Who?"

"Oh, isn't it wonderful?" Peter is dancing with joy. "She's near enough to come home tonight!"

The Mayor comes running, barefoot and puffing. "Wonderful?"

The mothers, next, cry, "Wonderful?"

And the whole crowd roars together: "Wonderful, yes! Because that kidnapper will not escape a second time!"

"No!" cries Peter. "No, everything is well with her! He hasn't hurt her at all."

"*He* hasn't? *Who* hasn't?"

"Why, the Troll hasn't," says Peter, grinning still. "The Water-Troll."

For an instant the night is as silent as death, and Dorf is horrified. *The Water-Troll! In the Well Despair! The stories, the stories! The horrible stories!*

"You must understand," Peter speaks sweetly into the silence, "that my daughter likes—"

"AH-*HA!*" the Sheriff booms. "I knew it! I knew it! The Troll is green, and didn't I *say* that the mud was green?"

As the Sheriff shouts, so shout the men: "We knew it! We knew it! We were only waiting to be sure."

And as the men all shout together, the Sheriff grows bolder. "Shrewdly we found the muddy beast!" he booms, drawing his sword. "And bravely we'll dispatch him!"

Peter raises his hands and calls, "No! The Troll does not deserve—"

But bold men shout the louder: "We're saving our children!"

And the Sheriff roars the laws, the laws in his blood: "Evil given, evil gotten, right?"

"Right!"

"A slasher—" the Sheriff roars.

And the whole village answers: "—should be slashed!"

"A killer—"

"—should be killed."

And so it is that with torches and weapons, with fire and scythes and righteousness, the people of Dorf are gone from the village. In a mob they are marching the ancient path through the fields and the woods to the northern valley, to the well they call Despair.

But Peter's back is too bent to keep up with these citizens. He trails behind them, crying, "People!"

> *"Oh, people, how I wish you heard*
>> *My still more gentle word:*
> *Eliza isn't suffering.*
>> *She rather likes to sing. . . ."*

Part Five: Midnight, the Bone-Fire, the Ending

own into the valley rush the people, their torches dancing. Across the valley floor they fly, the lanterns whirling. They look like a swarm of burning bees. They collect at the Well Despair.

The stones of the well shine red in the firelight. Tongues of torch-flame lick the night air, and *whoosh!* goes a torch when one man whips it round his head, and *whoosh!* goes another, *whoosh!* when it is waved.

The people make a circle around the well.

"Troll!" cries the Sheriff, delighted to be mad and to be here. "Troll, come out of hiding!"

"COME OUT!" cry the people.

"You've had your day. You've done your dirty work. It's our turn now. Never again will the children go to bed afraid—"

"OH, YOU *TROLL!*" the people roar, all in a single and swollen voice. "OH, YOU *MONSTER!*" they cry.

"Come out!" commands the Sheriff.

"COME OUT!"

Nothing. No one comes out.

"All right, then I'll count you out," the Sheriff shouts. "One!"

The people fall silent.

"Two!" he cries. He waits. "I'm going to say three," he warns.

"HE'S GOING TO SAY THREE!"

But before the Sheriff can say "three," here comes Peter, panting, pushing his way through the crowd and pleading, "Wait, wait, Elisabeth's down there!"

"Peter, you fool!" the Sheriff shouts. "Get out of here!"

But Peter has already run to the center of the circle. "Elisabeth!" he calls down the well. "Elisabeth, it's Papa!"

"Grab him," the Sheriff commands, infuriated by the interruption. "Drag him away from there."

Men move in and pull poor Peter backward.

"Three!" shrieks the Sheriff. "One, two, *three! That means we're done with talking. That means it's time for wood for a fire. Three means burn the monster out. Threeeee!"

"THREEEEE!" roars the mob while it goes for branches. Twigs and tinder, limbs and logs fly through the air and land at the well. The pile grows high and higher with a hole in the middle as black as a chimney.

Peter is down on his knees, wailing, "Elisabeth!"

But nobody hears him.

"Troll!" the Sheriff roars with a new solemnity, "behold your ending!"

And *whoosh!* goes his torch as he whirls it round his head. Then *whoosh!*—he throws it. It loops through the air and lands on the wood, and a flame leaps up and races around the well to form a perfect, pointed crown.

Oh, the people are lurid and laughing now. Their faces are bright in the blazing flames: they're killing the killer. They feel like God.

And the flaming brands go tumbling down the well. And light is blazing in the dark home of the Troll. And Peter hears a distant howl of mortal pain. He covers his mouth with his hands. That howl arises from the well. Elisabeth? Or who—?

Then something else is rising within the crown of fire. Something hunched and dark. *Look! Look!*

The valley is hushed.

For the Troll is coming up.

Slowly, slowly, out of the hole, an arm and a shoulder move like shadows inside the ring of flames. A head, a face, a terrible frown. The eyes are open, green and piercing. With cat feet the Troll steps on the glowing stones. He stands awhile, holding a bundle against his breast, wrapped like a babe in his long, damp hair. He crouches, hunch-backed, singed and smoking. He flares his nostrils, sniffing, sniffing the wind. And though water flows from his green eyes for the light and the pain, he looks, and he finds Peter.

Peter.

Now the Water-Troll bows down. He tucks the bundle beneath his chin and begins to pass through the fire itself, walking on the bright red branches. Fire and light are eating him.

Oh, what a hissing his passage makes! But he neither rushes nor stumbles. A bitter white cloud flows up from his body. The tears flood his green, green eyes—but he does not groan.

Down to the ground he steps. Across the grass he walks toward Peter, leaving scorch-prints behind him. He kneels before the weeping man. Gently he unwraps his hair, and there is Elisabeth, safe and pale and crying, too—and that makes three in tears.

"Canst thou hear me, Bonnie Lass?" he growls. "Canst understand me, Beth?"

The child doesn't move. She's gazing at a dying Troll, and she is grieving.

"Nay, Beth. Nay, don't cry," the monster murmurs.

Then all at once the Water-Troll ceases his perpetual frown and starts to smile. It is as though the most wonderful thought in all the world has just occurred to him. He reaches to the smoking hair on his head and one by one draws forth two objects.

"Thou gavest me a gift," he growls, "that someone first gave thee. This someone never lied to thee, Beth. This someone never left thee when thy mother did, but loved thee always, and always grieved *with* thee. Thy loss was his, thy hurt his own. Ah, don't the tears he drops tell me so? Nod, Beth. Nod thy pretty head for me."

The poor child, her tears streaming, nods for the Troll.

"Aye," he growls, low and lovely. "Good," he says. "And now I return the gift to its givers, one and two—to thee and to him who loves thee well."

The objects which the Troll is holding are tortoiseshell combs. One he winds into the black hair of Elisabeth. The other he gives to Peter. They are a set.

Thus the Troll has thought his thought and shall never frown again. He looks on the child with an infinite peace, and now:

> *He combs her hair. He kisses her.*
> *"Thee be my Queenling, Bonnie Beth:*
> *God save thee from this day," he saith,*
> *Then breathes the next to his final breath,*
> *And hides his face in fur—*
> *Forever.*

Epilogue: Eliza's Song, Eliza's Secret

Sometimes in these latter days an old man and a young woman of midnight hair walk down the ancient path to the valley near Dorf, to a well whose stones are black. They go arm in arm, and they whisper to one another of this wonder: that ugliness can be so beautiful. Side by side they stand at the well.

The old man has white hair and short legs and a heavier hunch in his back. These come of age. There is a green glint in his eye. That comes of wisdom.

Sometimes they spy lizards slipping among the stones. They laugh.

And sometimes, because this well is still the source of all water, they let down a little bucket, then draw it up and drink.

But before she drinks, the woman tips her ear to the water. She holds back her hair and listens. The water whispers to her the fondest of secrets, and she smiles. For this is what she hears:

Thee be my Queenling, Beth.

Forever.

Water is forever.

> *Now Elisabeth sings "Alack-a-day"*
>   *As often as she may.*
> *And still she wears her glove of glass,*
>   *So doth the gentle Lass.*
>
> *For once a Troll did set her by*
> *For fear that she might sink and die*
> *Within the flames that leaped so high*
>   *Around his citadel.*
>
> *Elisabeth has learned to sigh*
> *The widow's lullaby—and why?*
>   *He loved her, truth to tell.*
>   *He loved her very well.*

Authors and Artists

Publishers tend to keep the artist and the author of a children's picture book apart. Editors and book designers communicate directly with the artist, taking into account the author's suggestions, certainly, but then offering their own directives regarding which parts of a story should be illustrated and what the illustration might convey. They're somewhat fearful that, should artist and author talk directly, the author would dominate, demanding that his or her own imagined vision *become* the pictures in a children's book. That can diminish the book, the published presentation, by destroying an important dimension of the book whole.

I agree.

There ought to be a creative equality between the author and the artist. Neither should serve the other; rather, both the word and the image should serve, each according to its peculiar form and craft, the *story*. For me this is one of the greater delights of writing: to discover an entirely new vision for the story I had delivered in words. It is in a real sense the fruit of a marriage: just as a man and a woman together produce the child which is *of* both, bearing characteristics of both, but which is its own thing, finally, detached from both parents and altogether the image of neither one, so the children's picture book bears characteristics of its two progenitors, artist and author, but becomes its own thing, the thing it could *not* have been if the vision of one "parent" absolutely dominated the other.

I recall being impressed—delighted!—by the choices Arthur Rackham made when he illustrated in the early years of the twentieth century. A full page might be devoted to a tree, to the *roots* of that tree: twisted, dramatic, taking a rough-knuckled grip on the stone and the earth and the forest. The tree as a tree was only tangentially related to the tale. Ah, but the mood of the tree, the mute force of its presence, the grizzled animation it lent to every natural thing—these served to drive the tale to new levels of complexity and effect, bearing the child along, for such art needs no analysis to be understood; it needs only to be experienced. And children can experience what they see. So the very *sounds* and *music* of the words found rhythmic companionship in the very *lines* and *colors* of the art.

"Art." I think of the best children's book illustrators as more than just illustrators: I think of them as artists. Their work does more than to reflect my work; they comment on it. And more than simply adorning my language, they offer the second half of an experience whole.

I have been remarkably fortunate in the artistic transformations that my children's stories have received over the years. Deborah Healy painted the pictures that attended *Elisabeth and the Water-Troll* at its publication in 1991. She created a green Troll of slant eyes, swept-back whiskers, lynx ears, a narrow blade of a foregoing nose. The effect was something between an animal of acute attentions and a human of confusions. He had a slick cat-like beauty. But if one—awaking as Elisabeth did in a strange place—had expected to see a man nearby, the bestial element in Healy's Troll would be terrifying. Her work put me in mind of a French film directed by Jean Cocteau in 1946, *La Belle et la Bete* ("The Beauty and the Beast"), in which the beast is an actor whose face is savage, but whose body moves with articulate grace. At one point the beast leans against a closed door; on the other side is Beauty, sleeping; all his animal desire is to enter and possess her, but his goodness restrains him; and the eloquent bend of his body expresses the unspeakable torment the victory of goodness causes in him.

Whether she intended it or not, Healy created an artistic allusion, even as the story makes allusion to several tales collected by the Grimm brothers and to a whole history of sacrificial love. Her allusion is more than ornament. It understands and makes visually manifest the very core of this story, an accomplishment that *requires* the artist. The author cannot do this.

Nor is it necessary (let me quickly assure you) for anyone, child or adult, to "get" the allusion. Readers don't have to know or recall Cocteau's film. Rather, the allusion imports into the world of this story whole new worlds from other arts and other artists. What once moved the artist (or the writer) can, in artistic reproduction (infused with that artist's own past experience), move the reader, too.

In another children's book of mine, *Potter,* published in 1994, the artist Daniel San Souci shows a father carrying his sick son down the stairs, the mother immediately behind. The boy is nearly naked. His left arm hangs loose, inert, his eyes closed, his whole person unconscious. I looked and looked at that scene when first I saw it, wondering why it had such a mournful effect on me. Then, suddenly, I realized what it reflected and remembered a particular scene which artists have been recreating for centuries: it's called *The Deposition of Christ.* It shows Joseph of Arimathea carrying the corpse of Christ down from the cross—and Mary follows behind in a mother's crush of grief. Ah-ha! San Souci painted the grouping which generations and generations of artists have refined, gathering into this one page an entire history of loss and sorrow. Of *course* it is moving, whether or not the reader recognizes the countless hands that long have shaped it.

Likewise, San Souci touches lightly upon another traditional theme of painters, most famously found in St. Peter's Cathedral in Rome, executed in marble by Michelangelo: the *Pieta*. In our book, *Potter,* his mother leans over her son in bed, dabbing his forehead with a cloth, while he . . . well, sleeps, though the posture and expression could be that of one dead. Even so, depictions of the *Pieta* are representations of Mary mourning over the body of her dead son, Jesus.

Now, *Potter* is in fact about death and resurrection. (For children ought not be sheltered from the event that they must learn even now—when they are most faithfully and spiritually limber—to face and overcome.) But it's a friend of young Potter's that dies—one whom we never see in the story. He has died aforetimes, off-stage, so that tender children needn't actually encounter the dying. Potter grieves the loss. And Potter himself grows sick unto death. But he doesn't die. He, in real effect, rises from the possibility of death and learns the joy that passes sorrow. Whereas my telling of the story could not repeat over and over again the presence of death, and whereas my words could not *announce* the resurrection to come without spoiling the plot's power; yet San Souci's art could do both, silently, compellingly, by reference to Christ's death (whatever the artist's spiritual inclinations), which not only holds the notion of death before the reader palatably, unconsciously, but also signals a glorious resurrection to come.

Art. And artists. I've been very fortunate over the years to have had extraordinary partners in the creation of these children's books.

Deborah Healy painted, too, the pictures for *Branta and the Golden Stone,* which follows next in this anthology.

Tim Ladwig, with swooping, soaring, breathtaking points of view, painted the pictures for three of my books so far: *Probity Jones and the Fear Not Angel, Mary's First Christmas,* and *Peter's First Easter.* His characters are flush with character, absolutely accurate to their historical circumstance, and completely engaging with subtle emotion, the tiniest twist of expression communicating whole universes of interior thought.

Page through this book to find the dialogue I've held with Kevin Kimber. Rather than rooting deeply in any particular story, he has taken on a different task: finding the continuing voice of the author as it changes and trails through many tales. This is by stories to look *behind* the stories to the character and the themes of a storyteller.

What a benediction upon an author's career: to have worked with artists of other crafts, other forms, other media; to bear babies with visual artists, composing musicians, actors on stage, dancers, film directors.

But in every case, let the author approach such companions with a perfect (but never an abject) humility. For unless one accords honor and wonder unto the other, no newness can come of the marriage . . . servility only. And an enforced servitude kills the art in an artist.

Branta and the Golden Stone

Part One: The First Winter

Once there was a girl who lived alone on the northernmost island in all the world.

She lived in a cottage by a lake. The lake was ice for most of the year and banked with snow. Her father had built the cottage several years earlier: two rooms and a fireplace, a table, a chair, a little window facing the lake, and in each room a little bed.

The girl had flashing black eyes and midnight hair tied back from her brow. Her neck was noble, her skin so dark it gleamed in the moonlight—and always she wore a snow-white scarf buttoned above her ears.

If she walked abroad in the snow, you could see her because of her dark skin.

If she walked abroad at night, you could see her because of her white scarf.

Her name was Branta.

And during the bitter days of one particular winter, she went walking often, often. She would leave the cottage and wander over the frozen lake exactly as the moon goes wandering over the sky. Branta was lonely.

Her father had died in the night of the very first snow.

He had been a big man once, with a wild white beard and tremendous arms for carrying firewood. Branta's father had always kept a fire in the fireplace. No matter how cold the winter, their cottage was warm and bright and lovely.

But then one morning the man remained in bed.

Branta knocked on his door. "Papa?" she called softly. "Papa?" But all she heard was a moaning, like wind in the trees. She opened the door and saw by his eyes that her father was very sick.

Outside, the day was gray, the air dead still. Snowflakes began to whisper at the window. They powdered and thickened the distance.

But Branta's attentions were inside. All day long she bathed her father's face. He seemed to be sleeping. He seemed to be dreaming and struggling with something inside his dreams—and for his sake Branta kept the fire bright and warm in the fireplace.

In the evening the wind began to blow, crying *Ooooooo* in the chimney of the little cottage. The fire cowered. Branta built it higher. And then she heard her name: *Branta?* she heard. *Branta, come sit by me.*

"Papa?"

She ran and looked. Her father was awake, half-lifting his heavy arm and beckoning to her. "Sit beside me," he said softly, sadly. "I have something to tell you."

Branta sat on the little chair and bent her noble neck.

He gazed at his daughter a while, then he closed his eyes and took a deep breath.

"You've never asked why we live so far north," he said.

"I never minded," said Branta.

"Once," said the man with the wild white beard, "when your mother and I were young and happy, I was called a *magus*—a wise man. I could read the stars, Branta, as if they were words on a page."

The man sighed.

"But then," he said, "I stole the Golden Stone, and it made me famous. It made me more than a *magus*. It made me a magician."

He uttered the word *magician* with a shudder and with such despising that Branta said, "Papa, why haven't you told me these things before?"

He opened his eyes. "Because I am ashamed of them. They made your mother sad. They caused your mother a killing sorrow. Ahhh."

"But then, why are you telling me now?"

"Because I must give you something before I die, and you must understand it."

"Die! Oh, Papa, please let's talk of other things. Here, let me go build the fire for you—"

"No!" her father commanded. He drew breath to keep control of himself. "No," he said more kindly. "Let the fire grow cold. Stay with me and listen."

Far into the night, then, while the fire dwindled to ash and the grey ash cooled and the howling wind surrounded the cottage with drifts of snow, Branta's father told his story.

"The most important message I ever read in the stars," he said, "was that a Baby King was to be born in a distant kingdom. When I told the news to your mother, she said, 'Go.' She said, 'Who else can read the stars as you do? Who else knows that the Baby King is coming? Go and welcome him. Go.'

"So my brothers chose spices from orient trees as gifts for the King, and I chose a stone of gold, and we traveled the deserts westward, and still the stars led us as by a holy hand.

"Finally we found the tiny child, and I knew at once that he was more than a baby and more than a king. He gazed at us from his mother's arms. He raised his hands and, young as he was, he blessed us, and we *were* blessed. My brothers put their spices on the ground before him; but I lifted my gift to the child himself. He reached and touched it. Branta, listen to me: where his finger touched the gold, it made a deep print; and the whole stone glowed hot in my hand, and I felt the power go into it.

"Branta, Branta, I never let go of the stone! And when no one was looking, I slipped it into my pouch. My brothers left their myrrh and their frankincense behind. But I . . . I brought the golden stone back home with me. I stole it with the fingerprint. I stole it for its power."

Tears flowed from the old man's eyes, but he would not stop. He kept on talking.

"Your mother was frightened when she saw what I had done. 'Take it back,' she said. 'It belongs to the one who left his print on it.'

"I said, 'But if the Good King touched it, it will do good for many people.'

"She said, 'Please, please, take it back.'

"But I didn't. I used it. And indeed, I did much good with it. For this is the power of the Golden Stone: to change people. It can make them whatever they want to be. In my hand it made sick people healthy; it gave sight to the blind; it caused the crippled to walk. And often I said to your mother, 'Do you see all the good I'm doing?'

"But she said, 'No, husband. I see only that the Golden Stone is changing *you*. Now you are what you always wanted to be, whether you admitted it or not. You are a magician proud and famous, and that is *not* good.'

"Your mother's words made me angry. So I said, 'Woman, be still.'

"She looked me directly in my eyes, and she said, 'Do you mean that?'

"'Shut up! Shut up!' I shouted. 'Woman, don't talk to me!'

"Well, then your mother went to the place where I kept the Golden Stone. She picked it up and placed it against her lips and whispered, 'You have your wish. It is my wish, too. I will never speak again.'

"What did she mean? What had she done? I refused to think about it.

"In the days that followed, your mother, your mother: Ah, Branta, your mother did not speak. But I continued my work with a newer and fiercer conviction. People came to me; people were changed.

"Did an angry man want to be fire to burn his enemy's house? Well, when he left me he was a pure white flame, and his enemy's house burned down indeed—but after the fire was out, the man himself was never seen again.

"Did a greedy man wish to be rain to get himself rich crops? Well, he became a wonderful rainstorm, and his fields brought forth abundantly—but in the dry days of autumn someone else harvested the crops, because this man had run in streams to the sea.

"Branta, child: are you learning the danger of the Golden Stone?" Her father shuddered again. He shivered as if he were very cold. "No, no, the Stone was only as good as the wishes the people wished. Evil wishes did evil things. And whatever a person became by the force of the Stone, that is the thing the person must be forever. There was no coming back again. Is the fire out yet?" he whispered. "Is the grating cold yet?"

Quietly Branta rose and went to the fireplace. "Yes," she said. "It is out."

"Your mother died in silence," the old man said. Branta could not see him in the darkness. She could scarcely hear him beneath the shriek of the weather outside. Her father sounded far, far away. "She was going to have a baby," he said. "She lay down in silence. In silence she bore a baby girl. And finally she had the complete fulfillment of her wish upon the Golden Stone. She left me in perpetual silence. In silence my poor wife died. Branta . . . you were that baby girl.

"Branta?" the old man called. "Branta, can you hear me?"

But she could not speak right now, because of her sadness. She could only nod her head.

Her father said, "Reach into the ashes. Do you feel something hard and smooth?"

Yes. She felt a stone the size of a sparrow's egg.

"Bring it here," he said, and Branta did. She carried to her father a stone of gold so pure it glowed upon their faces. In its center was a baby's fingerprint.

"After your mother died, I tried to find the King so that I could return his stone. But that was years later, and no one knew of such a king. So I went away. I came north, as far north as I could, and I built a little cottage, and I built a big fire to keep you warm, and I kept the Stone in the heart of the fire for purity and for safety, for it could be dangerous in your hands, and I loved you, child, and I tried. . . ."

The old man closed his eyes.

Branta waited for him to draw the next breath. She waited for him to explain what it was he tried. But he never did. He never breathed again. Her father's beard was like a cloud around his face. He was peaceful now. He was dead. And the wind outside was wailing. And the world was wrapped in white.

So that's why Branta lived alone by the lake. And that's why she walked abroad all winter long in loneliness. She was thinking of her father.

When the nights were still, she would button her white scarf above her ears and go forth like the moon. When blizzards struck the island, blowing and howling and piling snow against the cottage, she stayed inside, building fires bright and warm.

But every night, whether windy or still, Branta would gaze at the Golden Stone, which lay on her father's pillow, and consider the terrible and beautiful meanings of the Stone and the story her father had told her.

Part Two: Spring

The northernmost island in all the world is winter for most of the year. But finally there comes a brief spring season when the ice breaks and the water gurgles down to the lake and the flowers sprout green and grow blue and yellow and red.

And so it was that the winter of Branta's sorrow came suddenly to an end when company came to stay on her island a while.

One morning, while the water still dripped from the eaves of the cottage, Branta stepped outside and looked around. She thought that she had heard laughter, somebody laughing.

The lake was glittering, the hills sweet green, the sky both bright and blue; but there was nobody anywhere, nobody laughing at all.

All at once she heard it again: straight up in the sky, *two* somebodies chatting and laughing and telling jokes in nasal voices. *"Gaba-gaba-gaba,"* they chuckled.

"Who are you?" Branta cried.

And then, exactly as if in answer to her question, she saw in the distance two dark bodies, each with a finger-long point in front and streaks at either side, which Branta took for wings.

"Birds," she whispered to herself.

They began to spiral down toward her island, great birds with black faces and long necks, pure white markings at their throats, grey bodies, and wings of a powerful stroke.

"Why, you are geese!" cried Branta, and she raised her hands for gladness. "Dear geese, I hope you will land on my lake!"

And they did.

Down they sailed on outstretched wings—splendid, regal creatures. They made a circle over the water, then pulled up on the flap of a wing, bent their necks, put out their feet, skated on the surface, and sank and sat and twitched their tails, curving their noble necks. A long journey was done.

"Geese!" cried Branta. "Geese, tell me a joke, and I will laugh with you!"

But the goose and her gander only glanced at the girl on the shore, then paddled to the other side of the lake, where they chatted and groomed their feathers

"*Gaba-gaba-gaba,*" they said—no language Branta could understand, no joke she could laugh at. For geese are geese, and people are people. They can be neighbors sharing a lake, but they cannot talk or hug as fathers and daughters do.

"But you won't mind if I watch you?" Branta murmured.

"*Gaba-gaba-gaba.*" From their distance the geese didn't seem to mind at all.

Branta took comfort in that. Life had returned to her island. So the spring had been good to her, and she was glad.

Part Three: Summer

ll over the island flowers burst forth. Whole fields of yellow blossoms nodded and trembled in the breezes. Great fronds of fern bowed over a moist ground. Reeds and sweet grass grew long around the lake.

And the female goose built a nest in the tall green shade. Carefully, she laid six smooth eggs into the protection of her nest. Then she and the gander made comfortable cluckings both day and night, and Branta was filled with excitement. In all her life she had never seen babies before.

So then the eggs hatched. And here came six brave goslings, each a puffball the size of Branta's fist, all following their mother, peeping, charging the wavelets of the lake, and rowing out like tiny boats.

Now this was a joke that Branta could understand. She laughed aloud on the shore, and sometimes the baby geese looked directly at her, and then she laughed harder than ever—as if she knew their little hearts, as if she had the right to love such handsome babies.

But swiftly do babies grow up. Soon the goslings were gone, and six true geese had taken their places, six faces black and white, six necks as noble as their parents' necks, and six new voices calling *"Gaba-gaba-gaba"* in a laughter Branta could not share, in a language she did not understand.

The summer was passing away. Eight grown geese would be leaving soon. Branta began to prepare for the dismal days ahead, carrying firewood into the cottage as her father had done, and stiffening her heart for the loneliness soon to come again.

Part Four: Autumn

ut this was the northernmost island in all the world. Here the winter could jump ahead of its time and come so suddenly that even geese might be caught by surprise.

In the year after Branta's father died, that is exactly what happened. One night the summer died. And then, just two nights into the season of autumn, a storm tore down from the northern seas and beat against the cottage all night long.

When she crept to the window the next morning, Branta saw that the long grass was broken and frozen stiff under a rime of ice; the sky was low and blowing; and the lake had been lashed into a foaming black fury. The north wind blew and blew—and there, huddled behind a boulder bigger than they, were the geese!

"Oh, no!" cried Branta. "I thought you were gone! Dear geese, you can hardly walk in this weather. However will you fly?"

All day Branta watched the family from her window, but the wind didn't break and the geese didn't move. And then the night arrived in perfect blackness, and the wind blew so fiercely that the fire in her fireplace ducked and guttered.

On the second day of the storm it snowed. The lake remained a ruptured, boiling grey; but the ground grew thick with drifts, and the geese were swallowed up altogether.

"Where are you?" Branta called.

She buttoned the white scarf above her ears and ran out into the blizzard.

"Are you dead?"

She stumbled toward the boulder, which was sunken in snow.

"Please, please, don't die!"

Branta reached into the snowdrift and touched warm feathers. Immediately eight geese burst up in a shower of snow and began to race away from her. Branta chased them.

"Wait!" she yelled. "I want to help you!"

But they were afraid of her. They were as scared of Branta as they were of the storm. When she ran at the goose, the mother of the children, she opened her wings to fly, but the wind slapped her backward, and she rolled like a ragged snowball along the ground. Branta tried to grab the tumbling bird, crying, "Come with me! You'll die out here!"

But it was no good. The goose rolled and ran farther and farther away, while the gander hissed at Branta, threatening to attack.

Branta had sad visions of eight geese frozen in the cold, their black eyes closed or clouded. Yet whenever she drew near to the children, they ran faster and farther away.

Well, she thought, *if they're afraid of me, maybe I can scare them into the cottage.*

Branta began to wave her arms and to scream louder than the wind. "Go! Go! Go!" she screamed—and for a while it worked. The goose and her six children ran in front of her, straight away from her; so she aimed them toward the door of the cottage, the warmth of the fire. But at the last instant the gander—close to the black, thrashing lake—cried, *"Gaba-gaba-gaba!"* and the whole family veered off in his direction, racing toward their deaths.

"Oh, you stupid geese!" Branta wept. "The cold will kill you, don't you know?"

But *"Gaba-gaba-gaba!"* the gander called, and him the geese obeyed. His was the language they understood. He was the one they trusted, even if it killed them.

And suddenly Branta, watching the young ones fight through the snow to their father, knew exactly what she was going to do.

She walked into the cottage. She knelt before the fireplace and heaped plenty of wood upon the fire, making sure it would last a long, long time. Then she rose and went into her father's room.

At his bedside she reached for the Golden Stone upon his pillow, and she held it in the palm of her hand, gazing at the tiny fingerprint.

"Baby King," she whispered, "I want to be a goose."

Branta touched the Golden Stone to her lips. Then, swiftly, she placed it upon her tongue. It was small. It tasted like spices, bitter as myrrh, and she swallowed it.

For a moment she kept her head bowed in silence. Then a fire ignited in her heart. It grew. It became a blaze. It coursed through her veins to the surface of her flesh, and she bent down, she bent her long neck down—and when she raised it up again, Branta had become a goose, a bright and glowing goose, for the heat went out from her body into the air.

Now she returned the way that she had come. She took short steps, silly and waddling steps, out into the storm—and the cold did not sting her anymore. She walked through drifts toward the lake, calling, *"Gaba-gaba-gaba!"* Close by the clapping lake she saw the geese. The tips of their feathers were white with ice. Some of them had already tucked their heads beneath their wings, preparing to sleep and to die.

"Gaba-gaba-gaba!" Branta called, running toward them. She nipped the backs of their necks. *"Gaba-gather-gather!"*

It was the mother of the children who pulled her feet out of the snow and began to walk to Branta. Here was someone exactly her size and her shape, someone with the same markings, black and white. Of course! What goose would not follow another goose who knew what to do and who spoke the same language after all?

The gander, whipped by the blizzard, cried, *"Gaba-gaba-Branta!"* He called her by name! *"Good-for-you-ba-Branta,"* he said. And then he was the last of the family of geese to follow her into the cottage. And there they all spent the third night of the storm, near a fire both bright and warm. And so it came to pass that they all survived.

Part Five: The Second Winter

When finally the storm abated that year, and the sun returned to beam warmth back into the earth, a small flock of geese flew up from the northernmost island in all the world. They formed a perfect V and turned to the south. It was very late in the season to be leaving, but these geese were no less healthy nor weaker for that.

Soon they were gossiping and telling jokes. Soon they were laughing, as do all geese when they travel.

"Gaba-gaba-gaba," they said.

There were nine in the flock: six children flying their first flight south, a mother goose and a gander, too—and one that once had been a girl, Branta, laughing as freely as any of the others.

For this was the truth of the Golden Stone, the length of love and the fullness of sacrifice: that whatever a person chose to become, she would stay that way forever.

The Writing of Branta and Other Affections

One: Wild Things

Maurice Sendak once told me of the furor that followed the publication of his children's book, *Where the Wild Things Are*. By pictures and elementally simple language, the story follows a small boy to bed, and then into his vivid, funny, and sometimes disquieting imagination as the bedroom itself morphs into a terrible woods and frightening creatures appear: the wild things. Many parents and some reviewers were downright upset that small children would see such stuff. They believed it would damage the children, implanting frights and fears in innocent brains, inspiring nightmares. Sleep? Sendak hath murdered sleep.

But the book prevailed, Sendak told me, because the book was right. It was the tender-hearted parent, the hyper-solicitous reviewer that was wrong. Far from inaugurating fears in children, such books as his gave a habitation and a name to fears the children *already* experienced, but amorphously, perplexedly.

One of the most important commandments for the creation of an effective children's tale is: thou shalt not condescend!

Adults who write to their *image* of a child, rather than writing to genuine children, do in a real sense utter baby talk. And they miss the mark of a child's intense experience. They make a conventional assumption of pastel innocence, angelic goodness, fresh unsullied souls ("trailing clouds of glory do we come/From God, who is our home")—and in consequence their language lisps, their menu of topics is reduced to the sugar cookie, and their attitude is offensive. Even as they presume to know better than the child, they present a teller and a tale too simple and simply *less* than a child can (and ought to, and wants to) experience. Simpletons tell simplistic tales.

But in fact, as Maurice Sendak knows and has demonstrated over and over (*In the Night Kitchen, Outside Over There*), stories can embrace all of the basic truths of this existence. They can confront every form of difficulty (Remember? Remember? Don't you remember the thicket in which you lived as a child?) because children are already experts in difficulty! And having both acknowledged and named the difficulties which children had only callowly *sensed* before, the plots of these stories can carry the child *through* difficulty toward a blessed, credible conclusion. And such conclusions to plots are, as you know, solutions to problems, now discovered not in rational explanations, but in experience.

Two: The Robber under My Bed

Let the adult write stories to the child *he* was and *she* was years ago, to the interior of that child, where emotions once spiked and sank with extreme—not to say "world-shaking"—intensity. For what child does not already know fears as doomful as darkness and the void? What child has not felt soul-pangs of guilt? And jealousy? What child has not laughed with such a helpless delight that heaven was surely at hand?

William Blake wrote two sets of poems, not so much for children (though children are quite able to receive them) as *about* children. The first set he called *Songs of Innocence*, from which, this example:

"*'Twas on a Holy Thursday, their innocent faces clean*
The children walking two & two, in red & blue & green . . ."
(from "Holy Thursday I").

The second set, which matches the first in titles, but contrasts it in vision, he called *Songs of Experience*:

"*Is this a holy thing to see,*
In a rich and fruitful land,
Babies reduced to misery,
Fed with cold and usurous hand?"
(from "Holy Thursday II").

Blake was well-aware that a child's heart knows both delight and despair, but knows it mutely (lacking a language to frame, form, or confront it). Knows it lonely (if no one can companion the child through the halls and tunnels of her interior life). Knows it meekly and weakly (because, without a name for the experience, the experience is much larger than her own powers of control and survival).

But it is the well-told story that can lend form and companionship and a name to the raw, inchoate experience!

By *story* the child might survive—particularly because story does not move by the cold calculations of reason, but rather by the swift and sensuous experiences of *imagination*.

So let me tell you the story of a story—and of stories in general, how they work. For when I was young and very young, I had already begun to "story" my universe, and by the force of imagination (by the shape of this storying) to make some sense of it. This is the writer's craft and the child's natural response, the child's native ability; child and artist *both* draw, by the same sensitivities, upon the same resources. There is a kinship here which rational thought and analytic adulthood can cancel. But the child *alone* with his imagination lacks (as the following example illustrates) one essential for the safe, persuasive conclusion of the story-experience: an *external* storyteller, a companion of love and authority to validate the imaginative flights of the child.

Once upon a time, when I was six—in the autumn of the year when I was in the first grade and walking some distance to and from the schoolhouse—there was a robber under my bed.

This is, as the best of stories always are, the truth.

Every night when my brother and I ascended the steps into our attic-bedroom, I knew with dreadful conviction that the robber had already secreted himself beneath our double-bed mattress. Such knowledge caused in me several sorts of torment: for my own skin, should he reach up and snatch me, yes. Of course. But that was the least of my worries. I worried rather more for my brother Paul, one year younger than I and completely oblivious of such proximate horrors; and I was in a state of trembling responsibility for the rest of my family. Robbers destroy. They can, of a sudden, break out and kill everything a small boy loves.

I was the oldest child of four-and-a-half children. I had been given the name of my father: Walter, as he was Walter. I was the only one in day-long school. I was the only one aware of the robber. Upon me, and upon no other, had fallen the task of preserving my family alive. *That* was the greatest torment of all.

The attic in which we slept was an attic. Dad had built walls into it, hiding the darker corners and the insulation and the rib-like trusses; and then he had said to us, "Your new bedroom." But we knew better. It smelled like an attic. The ceiling slanted as low as attic ceilings slant. There was one window at the far end, small and slashed by branch-shadows in the night: 'twas an attic. Where else would a canny robber choose to hide? Surely not in warmer bedrooms below. Rather, in the alien spaces, in the hedges and the fences at the *edge* of civilization: in otherness.

I was, it must be recorded, not altogether without advantage. I knew the rules of the game. For example, I knew that the robber was there, but the robber didn't know that I knew. Nor would he, if he could possibly help it, reveal himself to me—in which case the jig would be up, and though he might rush a-slaughtering through our house, he'd never get anything for it. Therefore, as long as I played innocent—and as long as I stayed *awake,* thereby giving him good reason to stay concealed beneath the bed—I could control the situation and preserve my dear ones alive. It was a frightfully dicey balance. It was, after all, a mortal game. And it was killing me.

Well, every night I made noise as Paul and I ascended the stairs. And I talked loudly, jovially to my brother while we changed into pajamas—as if all were truly well, and I was happy. (I spent energies, you see, in two opposing directions: upon my own private fears and stratagems and also upon a false, huffing happiness.) And once we were in bed and in the dark and watching the choppy-fingered shadows upon the window, I told Paul stories. I continued the stories until he fell sweetly asleep. And then I forced myself even then to talk, to talk, and so to keep the robber in hiding and my family out of danger.

But a child can keep up such midnight watches only so long.

And then he cracks.

One evening in October, my mother said, "Time for bed."

Paul cheerily began to trot toward the door and the stairs to our attic.

I, on the other hand, astonished myself by saying, "No."

I, in my extremity; I, at my wit's end, spontaneously and in genuine anguish, said, "No, Mom. No."

"What?" said my mother who, being unused to disagreement, was herself somewhat astonished. "What did you say?"

"I can't, Mom," I said. "We can't. We just can't go to bed."

"Yes, you can," she said, her eyes flashing. I recall that she was sitting in a living room chair at that moment. "And, Wally, you *will!*"

She didn't understand, of course. But her not understanding would be the death of me. I broke into tears.

"Wally?" she said, more softly. "What's the matter?"

"Oh, oh," I sobbed.

"Tell me," she said.

And I told her. I said, "There's a robber under our bed. Every night, a robber—"

"Oh, Wally!" Mom expostulated. "You know better than that."

"No, Mom! No!" I earnestly argued, opening my eyes wide. "There *is!* He's there right now."

Mom looked at me a moment. Then, abruptly, she stood up. "Come with me," she said, and marched toward the attic door.

Oh, how my heart kicked and blamed me then! My mother is a bold woman. Mostly, that was good. But this time it could cancel her.

"Mom! Mom! You don't understand!"

I raced after her. I would have run up the steps first, if I could have. But she was the swifter. Up the steps she strode, I rushing behind. But when I reached the top of the staircase, she was already at the side of my bed, bending at the hips. She reached, took hold of the bedspread, then, in a grand, dramatic motion—and with a cry of "See?"—she snatched spread and blankets and sheet off the bed entirely, opening the under-bed caverns for my inspection.

Slowly I bent, too. And I saw: dust bunnies, comic books, junk—and no robber . . . *that* night!

Paul was staring at me now. The boy at five had just encountered two explanations of a serious sense of trouble: our mother's rational and evidential "proofs" of its absence; and my "storied" version, which acknowledged its reality, but which at the same time offered some slight advantage to the kid who knew the rules.

Which do you think he would believe? Well, the question is better put: which *form* was more congenial to his child's mind? Yes: mine. Yes: story, because children solve problems by imagination, by giving personalities, person*hoods* to the abstractions they cannot otherwise understand.

Therefore, Paul and I were together convinced *not* that the robber did not exist, but rather that the robber was still watching outside the window, still waiting to clamber in.

Clearly, the adult method of empirical analysis neither persuaded us nor could comfort us. What it did accomplish, however, was the opposite of our mother's intent: it removed from us the best ally we might have had, an adult who would not only enter the premises of "story" as I, a child, had spontaneously begun to write it; who would not only accept this personification of evil; but who would also take upon herself the role of story *teller,* by plot and imagination to walk us through the evil to a sweet solution/conclusion.

For there *was* an evil abroad. There was an evil horribly near.

During my first year at school I discovered that I could no longer count on the goodness of other people. Nor could I, outside of my home's environment, always find a motive for the "bad" things they did. Laws were lost. Good order was exploding. For there was a fellow in the sixth grade, huge, his face blazing with pimples, who greeted me regularly with a punch to the solar plexus. And there was a widow-woman up the road whom other youths tormented mercilessly until—that very autumn!—she came walking down my street at night in her nightgown, confused, weeping, barefoot, and crazy. I never saw her again after that. Where did she go? And why would people want to hurt her?

Evil had entered my life. The shards and pieces of evil, miserably disconnected. Evil which, should it invade the consoling home, could destroy those dearest to me. A bewildering evil before which I was completely helpless. Ah, but I could—this nascent storyteller could—invoke fantasy to "story" it! And I did: I embodied formless evil in a figure, the robber; and I wrote into my story (what the credible universe of any story must have) contingent rules of action, by which rules the major character of the tale (me, of course) could find *some* advantage over evil after all.

Mom's methods did not solve the problem.

Nor can the children's story which refuses to acknowledge evil in a child's life solve the problem it will not name.

But the story that attends to the real problems of the child's existence can solve them, precisely because it *is* a story, and only a story. Fairy tales are a "safe" way to live through difficulty, as all the horrors are present and apparent and suffered—but only fantastically, in imagination. In imagination, too, they are overcome.

On the other hand, the tools of the triumph are often discovered within the hero of the story, with which the child-listener of the story is invited to identify. That is to say: the *tools* are not merely fantasy; they are real characteristics heretofore unrecognized by the child, now brought forth into his consciousness and placed into his hand as a real-world advantage when he encounters real-world problems. Hansel and Grethel discover bravery, trust/trustworthiness in one another, and cleverness, by which they triumph over the witch that would eat Hansel for dinner. And the child listening to the tale (who may have already experienced the fears of being abandoned by his or her parents) now *experiences* the power of bravery and trust and planned cleverness. And Branta learns the power of a self-giving love (which is the real and deeper tool represented by the Golden Stone). And these tools, as I say—being discovered in one's *self*—are not themselves merely stuff of fantasy. They are real. And they are the child's ever thereafter.

Only so long as the tale-teller is an adult who sees *more* than her child had seen in himself!

Moreover, the very form and the plot-order of the story becomes a map through some very real thickets of difficulty yet ahead for the child. And the value of this map is that it was drawn in experience, not in merely rational explanations. Explanations fail because they are printed on the brain alone, after which the child must labor to recall them and revise them to new circumstances and apply them. This is the problem: that the *child* must, perhaps when she is weakest, labor toward her own solution. But experience is printed upon the child whole; mind and emotion and senses and affections and fears and delights, available even to spontaneous action and response—for the child has been here before, has acted suddenly and passionately to meet this difficulty before, has laughed in victory before, but all in imagination.

In other words (and to use another, more substantial metaphor) the child has uttered the name of this thing before, knows its name by heart, and can control and command by the use of that name.

Three: A Local Habitation and a Name

In the Book of Genesis, chapter thirty-two, the patriarch Jacob returns to the land of his birth afraid to meet his older brother Esau, from whom he had usurped both his birthright and his father's blessing. Twenty years before, Esau had sworn to kill him. Now Jacob seeks to appease his powerful brother by sending ahead of himself all his goods in waves and waves as gifts for Esau. (Look how rich he has become! And look how generous!) Over the deep gorge of the Jabbok, Jacob sends all his cattle, all his serving people—even his wives and his children. And now it is night. And now the man named *Jacob,* the "Trickster," the "Usurper," is alone.

No, not altogether alone. "And a man wrestled with him until the breaking of the day."

A man: much more than a man.

That wrestling match must have been titanic, because the patriarchs of Genesis were considered to have been both mighty and massive. (For didn't Jacob use a stone as his pillow once? And wasn't that stone still there for people to see—a monument immovable?)

"Let me go," that figure says, "for the day is breaking."

Such seeming fear of the daylight makes Jacob think he's wrestling a night spirit—some sort of divinity, one powerful enough to have put Jacob's hip out of joint. Therefore, at one point Jacob makes a most telling request:

"Tell me, I pray, your name."

Why the name, particularly?

Well, in those days it was believed that numinous beings surrounded human beings invisibly, with extraordinary powers to determine their lives, but from whom the humans could not by their own strength free themselves. (This is not unlike all the forces that children believe to exist in their worlds, the Sendakian "Wild Things" over which, when yet unstoried, the children have no power, but which affect them personally and specifically.) Now, if one of these spirit beings became visible, became tangible in the visible sphere of life, where humans themselves lived; and if the human who encountered it could learn its *name,* then (1) that human learned also the spirit's nature and its intent; and (2) that human could, by uttering the name, summon it, obligate it, command it.

In fact, Jacob is wrong. This is no mere spirit of the night. This is the Lord God (with remarkable love paying attention to a single human), who does not permit his mystery or his freedom to be touched. Therefore Jacob's opponent deflects his request with a rhetorical question: "Why is it that you ask my name?" and refuses to give the name till much, much later.

But I tell that story here for the value of Jacob's presumption: even as he might have reversed his relationship with a spiritual (bodiless, powerful, amorphous) being by learning its name and thereby taking command, so children can (truly!) reverse *their* relationships with the powers which *they* believe to surround them by learning the names of these powers; by learning the name of the experience of one's encounter with these powers.

And stories *are* such names! The stories whole, I mean. And not the mute words printed upon a page, but the *experience* of the child who enters the tale and lives it: this is, altogether, in all its parts, the name.

Oh, and there's one other element I want to take from Jacob's tale. God (for God it is that wrestles with him), also asks Jacob for *his* name, and Jacob complies: "My name is Jacob, the Trickster, the Usurper." Then God the Creator, God the Wrestler, changes Jacob's name, thereby giving Jacob a whole new identity—and making the man also intensely aware of his identity: "Your name shall no more be called Jacob, but Israel, for you have striven with God and with men, and have prevailed." *Israel:* a pun, one who strives "with" God—both *against* God, and *beside* God, on his side.

My point is this: that the child who engages as fully and as personally with a story as Jacob here engages with the deity at the edge of the Jabbok (both wrestling and answering questions, talking, dialoguing) may, like Jacob, discover a piece of her *own* identity, and call her *own* self by name. To identify well with a major character in a story *is* to identify oneself.

Having established the paradigm of story as a name and a naming, let me offer a more particular explanation of how it works for the child. I'll develop this paradigm by further reference to the book of Genesis and the Hebrew notions of language implied in the creation narratives of chapters one, two, and three.

"In the beginning God created the heavens and the earth" . . . by speaking them. God *spoke* heaven and earth into being. Recognize an elemental simplicity in this Hebraic record of creation: the divine utterance ("Let there be light") did not command, as if the light itself were a separate entity capable of obedience; nor did the divine word design light or else manufacture it (in which case God's word and the light would be separate things, one the subject, the other its object). No: the word *was* the light! They were one and the same thing, "Light" and the light. So if, for example, a child were asked what the act of creating must have looked like, she might picture the holy mouth of God opening wide, then issuing forth a beam of universal light exactly as a song might go forth from the mouth of God into all the universe.

But the language of stark creation was only one of the languages which the Creator used. There are two kinds of divine talk remembered in Genesis, for what God had made, he also *named*. Light and its temporal period he called "day." Its dimming and the period of its absence he called "night." The firmament he called "heaven," the dry land "earth," the gathered waters "seas," and so forth.

Now, it is of crucial importance to understand that this naming did more than associate a particular sound with a particular thing (though modern societies use names as pointers merely, signs not much different from highway signs: *Chicago, 120 miles.* The highway sign isn't *actually* Chicago, of course: it says, "Chicago is that-a-way.") God's naming did more than produce the "word" by which speakers could refer to the object represented by that name. For the Hebrews, language was always an *action*. To speak was to accomplish. And to name a thing was actually to affect the thing named: it finished its creation, as it were, in three distinct ways.

1. The thing which is, but isn't named, cannot be known. If you can't talk about it, neither can you think about it or consider it or meditate upon it—nor, in consequence, can you know it at all! For the Hebrews, language is the stuff of knowing. Only when the created thing takes its place in language does it fully enter the realm of human awareness.

To name a thing, therefore, is to clothe it in visibility. To name a thing is to make it knowable, to grant its place in the human conception of the world. It *seems* suddenly to appear, that which had in fact existed before its appearing.

(But this concept is not restricted to the Hebrews. Most primitive cultures took time and tremendous pains to discover the *true* name of a child in order to present that child truly to the world—and to itself!)

2. That which is granted a name is thereby joined to the whole "grammar" of existence. As words are joined to words in the structure of a sentence, so any single thing named stands in a living and relational union—stands in a sweet kinship—with every other named thing in the universe. And as one word may enjoy an infinite variety of grammatical relationships, sentence to sentence, speech to speech; as the *changings* of relationship indicate the healthy flow of its life, so the thing named (or the person named) may enjoy the development of countless relationships to the grand creation of God.

3. And, finally, the name of a thing also contains the purpose and the value of that thing. It offers continually a *why,* a reason for this thing's participation in the fullness of creation. (Recall Jacob's new name, "Israel," and its effect on the man himself, changing his character, announcing his new purpose as a "Striver with God." "Israel" next became the name of a nation, God's chosen, holy nation: "A kingdom of priests to me," says the naming God in Exodus 19:6.) If the second effect of naming was to place it into the *space* of the world, this third effect places it into the *time* of the world, making it active, defining characteristic goals to be accomplished in the future. The named thing is an esteemed thing, for that it *serves* the whole.

And when God had created everything; and when the Lord God had assessed all things as "Good, very good"; and when humankind, in the image of the Creator, had been set as steward in the midst of all good things, then God granted unto us . . . not the first and primal tongue, to create out of nothing, but rather the second significant tongue: to name! And in naming to accomplish all three of the above effects upon the things and the people named.

So Adam was invited to name the animals, bringing them fully into his own knowing, establishing relationships with them and for them, discovering and applying purpose to them: that is to say, domesticating them.

But the highest thing the human could ever name was . . . another human. And so Adam and Eve did in the naming come to "know" each other, weave complex relationships with each other, affirm purpose and worth one upon the other:

> *Then the man said,*
> *"This at last is bone of my bones*
> *and flesh of my flesh;*
> *She shall be called* ishshah *[woman]*
> *because she was taken out of* ish. *[man]*

The Hebrew words *ishshah* and *ish* make the same sort of pun that the English words *woman* and *man* do: one word acts as a root for the other, longer word; while the shorter word needs the longer one for fulfillment. Man and Wo-Man need each other, both the names—the bare words—and the objects named.

Now, then, the application of my paradigm:

It is precisely this sort of naming that the story *is* and accomplishes for the feelings of children. The whole story—its full experience from "Once upon a time" to "happily ever after"—becomes the name of some previously nameless and shapeless trouble truly encountered in children's lives, a scary thought or mood discovered even within themselves, the fear suffered at natural transitions such as leaving home or going to school or finding a new baby in their houses or fearing abandonment by their parents. . . .

The story helps children to know what otherwise would lurk in the unknowable regions of their dark souls, or of the dark world. (This is what the "robber" story accomplished for me, giving my personal encounters with evil in the abstract a local habitation and a name.)

The story establishes effective, useful, healthy relationships with things now given shape. (Remember the rules young Wally understood to exist between himself and the robber—as well as the important relationships he, as the eldest, experienced with his family.)

The story even gives the children purpose and value, valor and strength, goodness and worth. (Hard as the responsibility was, I could nonetheless act as the savior of my family: I, I kept them alive!)

Now, therefore, what should we *not* tell stories about? What should we, therefore, *not* name for the sake of the children? Should we skip departures temporal? Departures mortal? Should Maurice Sendak *not* have given a name and a shape to the Wild Things of the child's perfervid imagination? And if he had not, what would that child have missed? Should "Branta and the Golden Stone" completely compromise this business of evil actions in beloved people (her father's selfish misuse of the Golden Stone)? Should Branta ignore the dyings that make us sad—and also, then, the sacrifice of love that makes us glad and good again?

The stories that contain badness are not bad stories. Rather, they are among some of the best. Because the storyteller who loves the children and gives the whole of his or her self to them by means of the tale—inviting at the same time the whole of the children's selves—is of all people the best able to confront true and truly terrible things *with* the children. The storyteller takes their hands and companions them into the future framed within the story, into the future awaiting them outside the story.

The storyteller who can name otherwise amorphous fears, does at the same time name the children! Knows them. Helps them to know their selves. Gives *them* place in the whole wide world. Persuades *them* of their value and purpose and strength and goodness and glory. Each may be, you see, a little Israel, if only the name has once become their experience.

So I wrote "Branta and the Golden Stone" with the hope of causing in children a love for Branta herself, by which love to identify with her—to dwell within her.

Branta should carry both bad and good into the children's experience; should name bad as bad, and good as good, and every child as loving of many things and filled with remarkable powers.

Branta knows loneliness in the extreme. So do children.

She has seen dying, and she has encountered the consequences of sin and greed and pride. A hard life? Yes, but no harder than the nightmares and the apprehensions of little children. And also as hard as life shall surely yet be for them.

But this is fantasy. This is the way children already think. And children distinguish between the experience of "playing at" something and the experience that forces itself upon them. They have control over fantasy! They can enter it just as far as they are prepared to experience it, and no farther. It is only as "real" as their hearts want to engage reality; otherwise, it's only a story. And the crossing of these boundaries is made possible and powerful when a loving, trusted adult journeys with them, arms around them, telling the tale or else reading the tale together.

Conclusion: Grasshoppers

ur son, Matthew, at six and seven years old dreamed horrible dreams. He would start from sleep, fly from his bedroom down the hall, then bullet his little body into *our* bed, eyes as wide as boiled eggs.

We could smell the fear on him, for it caused his sweat to sour.

"What, Matthew? What is it?" his mother would ask.

And he: "Grasshoppers!"

It was a recurring nightmare: grasshoppers lurked at the bottom of a hole in his pillow. Insects huger than himself. They bit, he said, "Sideways," and clacked when they chewed. They were waiting for the time he would fall down the shaft to their lair, where they would tear him apart for supper.

Three choices presented themselves to us, his parents.

But I had too strong a memory of my own childhood to make my mother's choice. No one would say to our son, "Oh, Matthew, don't be silly. There are no grasshoppers anywhere near your pillow."

On the other hand, I was probably still enough of the child myself to be stuck with the second choice: in a sense, I believed him.

Well, I began to dream my own dream, in which Matthew and I are walking over an endless field of grass, bright green, too perfectly green to be safe. Matthew worms his hand out of mine and dashes ahead. "Wait!" I cry. "Matthew, wait!" I cry with a deep parental dread of the dangers ahead of him. And sure enough, all at once he vanishes from my sight. He has fallen into the hole of *his* dream. I rush forward. I find the hole. I see him falling—and I see, at the bottom, the grasshoppers of the Apocalypse waiting to eat him, and now I am in unspeakable anguish for my son. Should I jump after him? Should I return for help? I wake up.

My wife made the third choice, the still more excellent way.

One night, having calmed him down, Thanne took her son's hand and walked back to his bed. She sat beside him on the bed and asked for the details of those grass-hoppers again. Matthew recounted them, whispering, terrified to mention them in their own hearing.

When he was done, Thanne said, "Is this the pillow?"—touching the one he slept with.

"Yesssss. . . ."

"Ah," she said, nodding in solemn agreement. "But," she said, "Matthew, did you know that grasshoppers, they are finicky?"

"Nooooo. . . ."

"Yes. Grasshoppers live in only one kind of pillow. This kind of pillow," she said, taking his from the bed. "Come with me," she said, and again she took his hand. She led him to a large garbage can in the kitchen, and there she stuffed the pillow good and gone forever.

Next, she got him a different sort of pillow, in which, she assured him, grasshoppers wouldn't be caught dead living.

Also, taking advantage of the opportunity, she removed all the toys he took with him to bed.

You see? Thanne companioned him into his story. She accepted its premises, but not its present ending. She assumed the role of the storyteller and thereby led her son through the terrible (and terribly true) terrain of the tale even unto a marvelous ending. Thanne uttered the whole of the name of the spirit that had come to wrestle my son night after night, to wrestle him in his solitude. So Matthew learned the night spirit's name as well. He took power over the demon.

And he never dreamed of grasshoppers again.

Solomon Grundy

1.

Solomon Grundy, an old, old man
With bald on his head and shake in his hand,
    Sauce on his clothes,
    Hairs in his nose,
Cripple in each of his digital toes—
Solomon Grundy was most impolite:
He died between Sunday and Saturday night.

Who knows where Solomon Grundy goes?
Or wither the soul of old Solomon blows?

His body is busy; the worms see to that:
From his ribs and his cheeks and the place where he sat
They're carting off cartilage, stripping the fat.
His body's beginning to decompose.
    But Solomon G!
    Oh, where is he?
Tell us where Solomon Grundy is at!

Who knows? Who knows where Solomon goes?
Who knows where his spirit intends to repose?

2.

Does it matter how Solomon passed away?
Perhaps it does, but who can say?

On Sunday the village was walking to church
For prayers and for praises, for pious research,
The women in crinoline, men in their vests,
Children, like criminals, dressed in their best—
When all at once Good-woman Brown,
The goodest widow in the town,
 Saw Grundy on his porch.

"Ay-eeeeee!" she screamed. She dropped to her knees.
"Oh, noooo," she groaned. She shivered and wheezed
 And fainted dead away.

"Good-woman! Good-woman!" the people cried;
They rushed to help her—and then they spied
The porch and its passenger, cold as clay,
The verminous Grundy, the Solomon eye,
 Defying their Sabbath Day.

Is he dead? Is he dead? O people, beware . . .
The old, old man was pale as prayer,
His eyes wide open, white with a stare,
His mouth agape as if words were in there.
(Oh, none durst touch Grundy, this sinister Sunday!)
Like a branch of the crooked hawthorn tree
His arm was raised, and the people could see
One finger pointing mournfully
 At them!
Ah, which is the secret the dead don't see?
And whose is the sin that will not be
 Condemned?

No, none durst touch Grundy that sinister Sunday.
He lay on his porch for the rest of the day
Till the knacker man came for to sack him away.
But how did he die? That no one can say.

3.

The sheriff did little. He waggled his head.
"Not to worry," he said, "since the dead are . . . just dead."
But no one believed him. They knew it by heart:
Dying is sometimes no less than the start!

And the preacher that Sunday, he preached about Grundy,
And sinners and Hell and the smell of wet bones,
Of souls lacking eyeballs, who stumble on stones,
Who weep for their rest and who creep into homes:
"Who knows," he preached in doleful tones
(While women made whimpers and men muffled moans)
"Who knows where old Solomon Grundy goes?
Whence or whither the soul of cold Solomon blows?"

Black Sunday! Slow Sunday, the hours full of woe.
Oh, ominous Sunday when nobody knows
What forces are fogging and filthing the air,
    Or who is going there. . . .

        While Solomon putrified
        People grew terrified,
        Cowered and occupied
            Heaven with prayer.
        Fathers were mortified;
        Mothers were mystified;
        Children ran off to hide
            Any-old-where:

In attics above; in cellars below;
In closets—*wherever* small bodies could go;
The children, they vanished. The children were gone.
Not a girl nor a boy, not a Jill nor a John
    For comfort or for care.

And so passed the daylight; and so came the gloom;
And so ticked the clock of unstoppable doom. . . .

And so came the night and the death-sweat, the dew.
Two owls took to flight and began to recite
The cold inquisitional question, *Who? Whooooo?*
Fathers might answer that; mothers knew "Who"—
Yet all of their houses stayed silent and still,
And everyone shuddered when one whippoorwill
Asked who was it whipping him, valley to hill:
    Who? Whooooo?

O Solomon, where goes your spirit and you?
Where do you wander? What mean you to do?

4.

By midnight the people were peering through blinds,
Through shutters and keyholes and cracks of all kinds,
Afraid to find something, yet seeking the signs
    That Grundy was on the attack.

And they weren't fools! These experienced spies
Saw something like fingers afloat in the skies,
Pinching the stars out like fireflies,
    And stuffing the moon in a sack!

And then, while they watched them, the fingers came down,
Caressing the rooftops, enclosing the town
In a grip of such darkness it cancelled the ground
    And buried the village in black.

This blackness was blacker than caverns or coal,
Blacker than smoke in the bottomless hole,
Than basements or Bibles or crypts or the crow
    That begs at the Devil's back:
        Black!

Solomon, Solomon, is it your soul
Or a cloud blowing over that makes us too cold?

Yes, midnight was thick. It was dim in extremes.
Then—suddenly!—wind hit the village with screams,
Both blasting the candles and shaking the beams
    And causing the children to wail.

Their mothers could hear them. The mothers could hear:
But no one could *see* in a darkness so weird.
"Jill! Jill!" they cried while the high wind jeered.
"Johnny! Calpernia!" Shaking with fear
    They searched for their children, but failed.
"Jimmy, where are you? Oh, Jimmy, I'm frantic!"
But Jimmy was stuck in a nook in the attic.
"My baby! My son!"—but her son had been swallowed
By nightmares more hateful and midnights more hollow
    Than Satan's Cimmerian jail.

Mothers and children were far, far apart,
Blackness between them, and sick in their heart.

Solomon, why do you do us this way?
Hath anyone harmed you? Did any betray
You or murder you, slay you for money in pay?
 Please, Solomon Grundy!
 Oh, let it be Monday!

And what of the men-folk? And where were the men,
The elders intelligent, soldiers belligerent,
Boastful, bombastic, magniloquent men?
Did the cries of the women mean nothing to them?
 No worries! No worrying!
 Listen: there's scurrying;
 Someone is hurrying,
Clattering, chattering, cursing, and BAM!
The fathers fly out of their doors with a SLAM!
The Toms and the Tobys, the Ralphs by the score,
The Jacks (and of these there were thirty or more),
The Dicks and the Dirks and the Peters all swore
To be bold in the blackness and ready for war:

Solomon Grundy, we'll get you somehow!
 We'll murder your ghost
 With a stake and a post
 In the shape of a cross,
 But much sharper than most!
We'll pierce you, your bowels, your heart, and your brow!

 The men?
So where were the men? In the roads. In the winds.
In the open, where fear ends and fury begins.
In a crowd. In a mob full of fists and foul grins,
Thick clubs on their shoulders, thin knives at their shins,
Hate in their gizzards, bane on their breath,
Prepared to put Solomon Grundy to death . . .
 Again.

"Ho! There he be!"
"Oh, no, he's not!"
"He's by that tree!"
"He's by that what?"
"Attack him!"
"No, wait—
    You fool, that's a *gate!*
That's nought but a gate swinging wide in the wind!"

    The men? Well, they battled.
    They clubbed their own cattle.
    They stormed through their orchards
    And killed their own apples;
They murdered twelve peck of potatoes—and then,
Lord, save us from Hell and from Grundy!—for then
Someone from somewhere began to fight them!

Such howling, such shrieking went on through the night,
For the men swung their cudgels with all of their might,
But someone swung harder: he knew how to smite!
        With terrible ease
        He battered their knees,
Their arms and their ears on the left and the right.
        He troubled their stomachs,
        He matched them their speeds,
        Tattooed them their skullbones,
        Disdained them their creeds,
And here's the advantage in all of his deeds:
    His doing was faster than sight!
No one saw *anyone* fighting the fight
In the deep of the dark, in the dark of the night
    In the night of old Grundy's despite.

Go, Solomon Grundy. Oh, get thee away.
The night is fast over. It's almost the day.
We've nothing to give thee, no words for to say.
We're beaten. Defeated. On favor we pray:
Thou, Solomon Grundy—please, let it be Monday.

5.

Well, Monday as always came soft to the town;
(If Mondays can laugh, well, this Monday fell down);
Solomon Grundy was nowhere around—
    But villagers, *they* made a sight.

In the streets were the fathers, asleep and reposed:
But Dick had his finger in Dirk's broker nose;
Dirk had a hold of the pants and the clothes
    That Jack had been wearing last night.

Now, the butt of Jack's club was in Thomas's mouth;
But Tom's club was gone; it had fetched such a clout
On Toby that Toby lit out for the south
    And ran till the dawn's early light.

The children? The children were tucked in their houses
In odd little corners like odd little mouses,
Curled in the closets on crinoline blouses,
    The places they hid in their fright.

Their mothers were stuck in the family commodes,
In ovens and chimneys, in chutes and small holes;
For who can chase children that wriggle like moles
    Through spaces both dismal and tight?
        Right!

6.

But Solomon Grundy, a dead, dead man,
Had died absolutely e'er Sunday began:
    He'd left the good town to its own.

For it would have been silly, disturbing his bones
To terrify folks with spectacular moans
       When, working together,
       They did it much better
       Than Solomon Grundy
       Could manage that Sunday—
And, bless them, they did it alone.

           Solomon Grundy
           Born on Monday,
           Christened on Tuesday,
           Married on Wednesday,
           Took ill on Thursday,
           Worse on Friday,
           Died on Saturday,
           Buried on Sunday:
           This is the end
           Of Solomon Grundy.

                —Anonymous

Sometimes Sound *Is* Sense

At its most elemental, language is sound. And sound, when it is broken into rhythm, has the delight of the drumbeat, the repetitions of natural and organic motion (pulse, tread, gallop, the snap of the jump-rope). And rhythmic sound, when it is shaped in the various caverns and occlusions of the human mouth, is melody.

For me, *Solomon Grundy* was first of all plain fun. Its sound (if not its sense) moves on the fundamental level of the nursery rhyme, which needs no other reason to be than that it is plain fun. The music of the mouth touches a child's ear with the same relational effect, I think, as a tickling pinch upon the child's toe: both can make even the wordless infant squeal with delight.

> *This little piggy went to market;*
> *This little piggy stayed home;*
> *This little piggy had roast beef;*
> *This little piggy had none—*
> *And this little piggy cried, Wee-wee-wee-wee,*
> *All the way home.*

That's the way I remember the rhyme, both receiving it as the child and giving it away years later. And I recall how the *Wee-wee-wees* caused the most laughter, though they make the least sense, being sound as sound alone—and being accompanied by sweet tuggings on the little toe. Both sorts of touchings are rhythmic and relational. It's a parent and a child being "We" together. That's all. No information is communicated, no lesson taught, no moral imprinted. Just fun. Just us.

But then, when the child herself begins to repeat the nursery rhyme over and over, I think the pleasure is not only in the ear, but in the mouth as well.

As much as any other part of our bodies, the mouth is a posturing organ. If we enjoy the rhythmic motion of arms and legs in dance—motion refined, but motion much for its own sake and for the beauty it produces—we may as well enjoy the mere motion (the complex, rhythmic, repetitive motion) of lips, teeth, tongue, jaw, voice box, and those bellows below, the lungs. And then *that* motion can both accompany and command the motions of the bodies of several children together: producing and controlling the communal dance. This, I think, is the delight of the rhymes the children say when skipping rope:

> *Cinderella*
> *Kissed her fella . . .*

Or, again:

> *John and Julie, sitting in a tree*
> *K - I - S - S - I - N - G;*
> *How many kisses did he get?*
> *One,*
> *Two . . .*

With that second rhyme comes the further complexity of shaping the sense *by* the music of the poetic line. Rhyme and rhythm, when they work best, are not a form unrelated to the sense of the piece. They abet the sense. For example, they can hold back an ironic punch line even while they keep promising the punch to come. The promise is in the repetition of one particular end-sound, a rhyme, *after* another sound has been established in the ear and waits its own repetition, its rhyme, at the punch. In the following nursery rhyme, it's the sixth line of each verse that holds the punch, after having been set up in the third; lines one, two, four, and five, all repeating the intermediate rhyme, promise the fulfillment of the sixth. *With* the sound at the end of the sixth, then, comes a distinct (and experienced) sense of completion:

> *The Queen of Hearts,*
> *She made some tarts,*
>   *All on a summer's day;*
> *The Knave of Hearts*
> *He stole those tarts*
>   *And took them clean away.*

The King of Hearts
Called for the tarts
     And beat the Knave full sore;
The Knave of Hearts
Brought back the tarts,
     And vowed he'd steal no more.

And you've already marked the next level of complication: that the nursery rhyme is now playing against real objects in the child's daily life, in this case a deck of playing cards. It all combines in one organic unity.

And so my fun with *Solomon Grundy.* I bind entire episodes together by the repetition of a particular sound at the ends of the shorter line, which itself ends verses in that episode. See the first four verses of the fourth part: the *ear* finds and retains the form of the episode of the descent of a dreadful midnight. See—no, *listen* to—the entire fifth part, shaped by rhythm and by rhyme. Notice, too, how jokes arrive with and by means of sound, as when, in the fourth verse of that fifth part, we suddenly encounter the children hidden away. Here, the end-rhyme suddenly shifts to double syllables, the second syllable the weaker, causing a sense of lightness and of tender humor: "In odd little corners like odd little mouses."

Though the content of *Solomon Grundy* is gruesome in places, its form, the sound by which it is delivered and received, merely whistles and winks. The music continues throughout to grin, taking all things in a spirit less than serious.

The *whole* piece, therefore, pokes fun at the foolishness of certain human fears—as well as the stupidity of certain human behaviors. It does so by the melody in the ear and the dance of the mouth.

Now, there are observations here, indeed, that children are not old enough to understand. There are complexities to the narrative and ironies in the language beyond a child's natural comprehension. So at some levels this is a piece which uses the tradition of the nursery rhyme for purposes beyond that tradition. Elements of *Solomon Grundy* work only for an adult's experience.

But a phrase like "Satan's Cimmerian jail" can nevertheless have as real an impact on the unschooled ear as "Hickory dickory dock" does.

And when I've read this story out loud to children, allowing my voice a fullness of portentous melody, giving my face expressions to match the extremities of rhythm and sound, they have always been able to track with it on an emotional level, even when the intellectual was too obscure for them. Children can see and feel and experience an image. Their hearts can dance to musics that their minds may not interpret. And they can mimic what they may not understand.

"Who is silly?" I say to the children.

"You are silly!" they cry back.

"And Solomon Grundy, is he silly?"

"No! He's dead!"

"Then who is silly?" I say.

And they throw back their heads and shout with a bold and giddy hilarity: "The daddies! The mommies!"

Right on. Adults are silly. Silly. Silliest.

When Mother Commanded My Brother and Me to "Clean Your Room!"

I swept my room
With a mighty broom.
I scrubbed my floor
Two times and more,
Crammed shirts and shorts
In dresser drawers—
And stuffed my stuff in the closet.

I smoothed the creases
From my sheetses,
Pulled the covers
Up and over,
Threw my pillows
Out the windows—
And jammed my junk in the closet.

Dodged cobwebs with
 Agility,
Squashed spiders, killed
 The millipedes,
Broke roaches at
 Their little knees,
Then stuck each corpse
On a dinner fork—
And crammed them all in the closet.

Books and boxes
 In the closet;
Broken clockses
 In the closet;
Frogs and polliwogs,
Fish and puppy dogs,
Toenails, baby-teeth
Combs and bridal wreaths,
 Sandwiches,
 Handkerchiefs,
 Cookies and
 Candlesticks,
 Balls and
 Dolls and
 Bats and
 Cat skins,
All of these, all of these, all of these, all of these,
Pushed and packed in the *closet!*

When mother came . . .
When came our mother . . .
Calling my name
And the name of my brother,
She froze in the doorway,
Shocked at the sight
Of *bright* in our bedroom,
Of *clean* and of *light*
And of *shine* on the door of my closet.

But, "Where's your brother?"
Asked my mother—
And the closet door said, "Help."

"Oh, where is my son,
The littlest one?"—
And the closet seemed to swell.

That closet, so loaded,
First groaned, then unbolted,
Then opened! EXPLODED
My stuff! My stuff!
My bugs and my junk
All over and under
        My room!

And *there* was my brother,
That little thumb-sucker,
The love of his mother—
As squashed and as puckered
     As prunes!

My mother's suspicious.
She frowned, then she switched us.
He got peach cobbler,
While she made my closet
   (Dark and hollow,
   And *locked* on a fellow) . . .
     . . . My tomb!

Lily

Once upon a time, long ago (*so* long ago, in fact, that the plants and the animals were only just beginning to know the grand, new world around them)—once upon a time, I say, three sisters lived at the southern edge of a northern forest, where the sun's good light could shine on them from morning to evening, every day of their lives. It was a busy, abundant place to live: squirrels and birds and mice and grass, the handsome trees all dressed in green. And the sun beamed down and blessed them all.

Now, the three sisters were plants of various qualities. The oldest was named Bean Plant; the second, Marigold—and the youngest of all was called Lily.

Bean Plant was plain. Her flowers in June were tiny purses, white and plain. But never mind her plainness, because this eldest sister, oh, how well she worked! She opened her leaves to catch the sunlight, as much of the sunlight as ever she could; and from the sun's light she grew beans. By July there hung from her arms a hundred beans, sweet, green, and as long as sausages.

"Food," said Bean Plant, proud of herself. "Someone who feeds the birds and the squirrels must be very important in the world, don't you think?"

Marigold, on the other hand, was beautiful. She said, "Hum," and "Oh, yes," and "To be sure: I am such a knockout for prettiness."

By August, Marigold had adorned herself in petals so golden and glorious that she surely outshined the sun, to whom she compared herself, often and favorably, proving her own importance upon the earth: for what is a world without beauty, after all?

Beautiful Marigold and busy Bean Plant both had good friends and fine reputations. They gave excellent parties. The grass and the leaves and the breezes danced with the one, while birds and squirrels came to a dinner prepared by the other. And everything about their lives in this fresh, new world *would* have been perfect—except for the presence of their little sister.

"Shut up! Shut up!" they said at least three times a day. "Lily, either shut up or go away. You embarrass us!"

For what did Lily have to offer the world? How was *she* important? This youngest sister had no blossom for beauty: just one green stem a little too thick, and flat green leaves a little too weak. Nor was there anything Lily produced; no, nothing the silly plant *did*—well, well—except to talk nonsense, which is why her sisters said, "Shut up! Shut up!" so much.

Unlovely Lily, she talked to the *sun,* whom she thought looked royal in his morning robes and his midday crown, whose evening dress so filled the sky with lavender, lilac, magenta, and mauve, that Lily could scarcely breathe.

Bean Plant said, "The sun doesn't talk. It warms my arms to make my beans; but fire, Lily, fire never *talked.*"

Lily said, "Maybe no. But maybe so."

Marigold said, "The sun doesn't talk. It shines to show off pretty things; but lights, Lily, lights never *talked.*"

Lily said, "Maybe no. But maybe so."

She never argued with her sisters. But neither did she stop talking to the sun.

July and August and September, every morning when he rose in the east, wearing his flaming robes and leaning on the edge of the earth, it seemed that his smile alone said, "GOOD."

And right away, Lily said, "Morning!"

And so they said *Good morning* together.

Every noon, when he looked down from the highest heaven and beamed his brightest blessing upon the earth, it seemed that his glory said, "GOOD."

And Lily on earth cried, "Day!"

And so they said *Good day* together.

And every evening after a wonderful day, when in orchid and perse and plum the sun knelt down upon the western horizon and stretched before he went to bed, he said softly, "GOOD."

But then Lily never said, "Bye." She didn't like the word *Good-bye,* because by now she loved the sun who looked at her the whole day long, who gave her attention and warmth and conversation. She loved the sun, and she wondered if he loved her.

Therefore, every evening she said, "Night."

And so they said *Good night* together.

And Lily slept well till the morning returned. And the sun.

⁂

In October, when Bean Plant's beans had dried to a fine crackle and Marigold's blossom was the goldest it ever would be; in autumn, when the air was cool and work was over for a while, these two sisters threw their bestest, most busy, most glorious party of the year. The squirrels and the birds and the mice all came. Everyone talked about fur coats and feather hats, of acorns and hickory nuts and grass seeds, of rich harvests and such abundance that the days could only get better and better.

The trees dressed in blazing colors.

The breezes danced with Marigold brisker and swifter than ever. They swung her beautiful bonnet around and around until she could almost have died for joy.

But just at sunset, just as the party was at its happiest, somebody started to cry.

Did I say *cry?* Oh, my, it was so much worse than that. Somebody started to bawl, to shriek and to boo-hoo so miserably that the party died right then and there. Everyone grew gloomy, and the two sisters were themselves embarrassed to death.

"Lily! Lily!" Marigold screamed. "Why are you crying?"

"Because of the sun," poor Lily said.

"The sun?" Bean Plant snapped. "The *sun,* Lily? What *about* the sun?"

Lily whispered through her sobs, "He's dying."

"WHAT?" the sisters howled together. "THE SUN IS FIRE! THE SUN IS LIGHT! FIRE AND LIGHT ARE *NOT* ALIVE, AND SO THEY CANNOT DIE!"

But Lily whispered, "Look how late he gets up in the morning."

The squirrels nodded. The squirrels agreed.

"And look how low he goes in the day."

The birds that flew admitted that this was true.

"And look there," Lily pointed to the tired sun upon the horizon. "Look how early he falls to bed in the evening, sooner and weaker and colder than ever. He's dying," Lily sobbed, very sure, very certain. "But he never yet did tell me," she wept, "if he loves me."

"LOVES YOU?" screamed the sisters. How stupid! How humiliating!

And "WAIT!" they cried. Their guests were beginning to leave. And the wind turned chilly. And the leaves were stiff and trembling. And, yes, yes, they all had been convinced by Lily—stupid, silly Lily!—that the sun was in decline.

"Wait," called Bean Plant. "Don't worry! Even if the sunfires go out, I have dried beans! I have food enough for a hundred days!"

And "Wait!" called Marigold. "It's okay! Even if the sunlight goes out, I will shine my own golden light for you!"

⸎⸎

But time—as it always does, no matter what we do—passed by.

The sun grew weaker and weaker.

Lily met him day after day, again and again and again. She listened to him as she had never listened to him before—and suddenly she realized that he had been saying another word besides the one word "GOOD." In fact, he had been saying this other word all along, once a day, every day, the whole day through, but she hadn't heard it until she began to listen with sadness and sorrow and yearning and the sharpest kind of loving. The word wasn't "GOOD," but it *was* a good word, a promise word, a word that made poor Lily very strong!

⁙

Finally, in grey November, a terrible, terribly new wind blew down from the north. This wind was as white as ice, as cruel as zero, and colder than the grave.

It tore all the leaves from the trees, leaving tree limbs bare and trembling, while the leaves themselves chittered and whispered: *The killer! The killer is coming!*

Now all the birds took to their wings, to fly south as fast as they could go.

"We cannot stay," they cried to the sisters. "The winds say the killer is coming, and no one is safe. For he kills," cried the birds in the terrible wind, "by *kissing!*"

Skinny Bean Plant burst into tears.

"Not fair!" she wailed. "All my life I've worked so *hard*. I've done what I should, and I have been good! I don't deserve to die!"

Right away Lily called to her and said, "Bean Plant, don't worry! All will be right in the end! The sun has given me one more word. He said . . ."

Bean Plant was crying, "I want to live! I don't want to—" when suddenly her voice was cut off and she was left silent, standing on one foot, quivering in the midst of a cold field, because the murderer had come. Winter had kissed her his cold and mortal kiss.

So Marigold started the screech: "She was plain, but I'm so beautiful! I'm a treasure, more golden than gold! What would the world do without me if I died?"

Lily called, "Marigold, it's okay! Dying's not so bad. The sun, he has spoken the most powerful word. . . ."

But Marigold was bending her head and burying it under the ground; she was whimpering, "I'm too pretty to—" when the cold kiss of winter came even through the earth and turned her golden petals brown and down and dead.

Now, then, Lily—the youngest sister of all—was angry!

"I hate you!" she screamed straight into the wind, straight into the teeth of winter.

"I hate you for killing my sisters, my sisters, my goodness, my beauty!"

Oh, Lily was strong now and free, and this is the truth: she was not afraid. She was braver than daylight.

"I hate you, I hate you, I hate you for killing the sun, the shining daybright sun! Any time you want to, you old curse, old winter, just come and kiss me, and see if I care!"

Well, and winter did just that.

Winter came and kissed her, too.

But Lily did not complain.

And Lily did not cry.

For she had heard the yet more perfect word. Quietly she lay down, and quietly she died.

But this is not the end of the story. It doesn't end with dying. Because winter is not forever.

When the murderer had done all that he could do, when winter itself, like time, passed by . . . then, in the fresh spring and in the sweet breezes, at the southern edge of a northern forest, there stood a flower strong and tall, with a blossom as purely white as the first light of the world.

Lily. The child herself. Alive.

And trembling within the rim of her blossom was a single drop of water.

Now, somebody might say that this water was a dewdrop, which would be the natural thing to say. But it would be wrong.

I'll tell you the truth: it wasn't the dew at all, not the dew of the morning nor of the evening either. Rather, it was a teardrop of perfect gladness.

For this is the word that Lily had heard all summer long before: *Again.* With every new day, *Again. As today, so tomorrow: I will come again.*

And, true to his word, the sun had come.

The sun had warmed the cold, cold earth.

The sun had come and kissed dead Lily lying underneath the earth. This is how he roused her. And this is how he said to her, *I love you, child. I do, and I have always, and I will always, love you.*

And who could resist such loving without a tear?

Not Lily.

Not me.

And I know this for a fact: not you, either. Neither could you.

To Weave a World

One: Snow White, How Story Interprets the World

hen I was a child, I spake as a child; I understood as a child. When I became a man I may have put away childish things—but the man I became was shaped in childhood, and that shape remains forever.

Fairy tales shaped me. I have since "put them away." That is, the adult is a mostly rational creature, aware that fairy tales are not "real," but are a fantasy, an entertaining escape from the problems of the real world. As a man, I make such tales an object of my attention and maintain an analytical control over them: I read them. I interpret them; they don't interpret me. I master the tales, placing them within my memory and my experience exactly where I wish them to be.

Fairy tales dwell within the adult.

But as a child all full of wonder I approached the fairy tale as something real indeed. Children meet the problems of the world (as we've demonstrated in a previous essay) not with their logical minds, but with their imaginations, and the fairy tale honors and feeds and abets the imagination. I accepted its invitation myself to enter *it*—and there I dwelt: within the tale which, in fact, *did* interpret me. As a child I felt the tale; I sank inside it; I lived its composed experience from "Once upon a time" to "happily ever after." I *lived* the solution to which the tale had walked me, the whole of me, my mind, my emotions, my senses, my bone, my self.

The fairy tale was like a well-built house which I inhabited safe and strong and significant. The problems outside didn't vanish when I entered the house; but its walls protected me from immediate danger.

More wonderfully, when viewed through the windows of the fairy tale, those "real world" problems shrank to proportions equal to my child's size, and I discovered marvelous ways to triumph over them. And the shape of the house (when it was truly experienced, primally experienced) became the shape of the exterior universe when finally I stepped outside again. By the art of the tale and by the power of my magic imagination, the tale that interpreted me had also interpreted and ordered the world around me. I became a citizen and a survivor in an otherwise confusing universe—and sometimes, even, a hero.

Real world problems? Seeking a storied solution?

Once upon a time, my mother was the problem.

She, the largest figure of my real world, was beautiful beyond my deserving, and I loved her. I, the oldest of all her children, would truly have died for her, could it assure her happiness. But things were not so simple, and I despaired of solving the problem of my mother . . . until a tale revised my comprehension of the world and persuaded me of the secret of mothers in general.

Here's the problem:

In an evening darkness my mother would come to tuck me in bed. At any time there was tremendous comfort in the experience. But on those nights when she had dressed to go out I grew dizzy in the glory of her presence, all my senses alert to her beauty. When she sat on the side of my bed, her weight dipped the mattress, and I rolled against her. I felt her warmth. I felt the coolness of her hand upon my cheek. I heard the murmurous quality of her voice. I smelled the sacred cloud of perfume that surrounded her.

"Good night, Wally. Good night."

She had midnight hair, deep red lipstick. We prayed together, and then she would lean down and kiss me on the center of my forehead. Woman of mystery, going forth to possess the night.

That kiss was a medallion, reassuring me. If I sought proofs of her love in her absence, I would slip from bed and run to the bathroom mirror, there to see the red smack of her lips upon my flesh. Yes. She loved me.

How many mornings, then, didn't I wander downstairs to seek my queen, forgetful of the problem which every morning I encountered?

Mother is in the kitchen, at the counter, stuffing lunch bags. Her bathrobe is snagged and ratty, her hair wild, her heels hard, her gestures abrupt.

"Mom?" I say, anticipating kindness.

No answer. Siblings are hushed. I should take the hint. I don't.

"Mom, do you know where my sock is?"

And she erupts.

"What am I, your slave? I should, what? You tell me, Wally: what should I do? Do everything for you? You're lazy and you're late!" Her cheeks are white with anger, her mouth stiff.

I say, "But—"

She snaps: "If you'd keep your room clean, you wouldn't *lose* your socks!"

"But, I—"

"Don't you *but* me, mister! One more *but* and I'm liable to—"

What my mother is liable to do is terrifying. She's liable to say, "Come here," then, "Take off your glasses," because she doesn't want to break them when she slaps me.

I *but* her no more *buts,* though I have several yet to go.

"You've got fifteen minutes, mister. If you're not dressed and ready in fifteen minutes, I'm leaving without you. You'll walk to school."

I don't find the sock. Trembling, I cannot find the sock.

My mother keeps her promise. I hear the car whining backward down the driveway, shifting, roaring off to school, while I sit on the side of my bed, filled with a diffused guilt, lonely in the universe.

When she returns and finds me sitting so, she drags the whole bed away from the wall and points to a spot between the wall and the bedpost. There is my sock.

I dress.

When I'm ready to go, my mothers gives me a note for my teacher.

Amazingly, I find my way through town to school.

The entire class turns to look at me when I creep in the door. I give the teacher the note. She reads it, then glares at me.

"So," she says, "your mother says you are not sick. Your tardiness is your own fault."

As long as my mother was unsolvable, so was the whole world an impossible complexity to me, and a dangerous place besides. Cause and consequence had no connections I could trust. I withheld myself from the treacheries of friendship. I listened to everyone, but spoke to no one.

Then one day the teacher read aloud a fairy tale whose fiction I genuinely entered, whose events I believed and experienced as my own, whose world resolved my own most troubled world—and (as a child, by the marvel of imagination) I did at last understand my mother. I was set free to love her again without fear.

Allow me to recount some of the details of this fairy tale; they are the images which invited my full experience precisely because they were familiar to me. They crossed both worlds, the tale's and my own. They became my doorway:

A queen sits in the casement of a high window, sewing and sighing. She sighs for the lack of a child. She yearns to mother a child. The casement is ebony black. A cold snow is falling, pillowing the sill in white.

As she sews, the queen pricks her finger. Three drops of blood print the snow with crimson.

"Oh, let me have a child," the queen prays to heaven. "Let me bear a child with lips as red as blood and cheeks as white as snow and hair as black as ebony."

It is absolutely certain this queen will love completely and forever. I know her. I know her perfume, and I give her my own complete devotion. And when God grants her the child of her heart and her prayer, I am not surprised: I recognize the baby, too.

But then the good queen dies.

And soon, too soon, the king marries another woman, a second one to raise the child who is as beautiful as the first mother was. But this mother is wicked. She talks to herself. And her Self answers from the depths of a mirror.

"Mirror, mirror on the wall, who's the fairest of us all?"

The image in the mirror answers, "You are," and the wicked mother is content—but only for a while.

Because, as the child grows, so does the child's beauty, until it surpasses the beauty of the wicked second mother.

"Who is the fairest?" now she asks.

And the image in the mirror responds with flat truth: "Snow White is the fairest."

Snow White: the child of the first mother, the godly mother, the one who died.

Oh, how the second mother howls at the knowledge, which must accuse her even as it diminishes her! Cheeks white with anger; a mouth gone stiff—I know this woman, too! I meet her often in the mornings, and suddenly I understand (as a child understands these things) her changes and her rages.

For I am Snow White, imprinted with the enduring, deep red beauty of the first mother forever, for hadn't *she* borne me, and hadn't she placed her crimson emblem upon me?

So this was the freedom that I carried back into the "real" world. (I am neither exaggerating nor fabricating for the sake of an argument; I am in fact reporting the genuine effect upon me which the fairy tale had, although I did not then reduce the effect to analytic words as I do now.) My liberation came in the fantastic revelation that I had not one, but two mothers. As I parsed it, I had a Mother of the Evening who loved me truly and well, whose beauty I shared, but who disappeared (died) not once only, but night after night. And I had a Mother of the Morning who possessed a different nature altogether, and who probably saw in me (the child of both) the beauty, the godliness and the goodness, of that other mother who was (well, *look* at me!) more beautiful than she.

Now, if the accusatory angers of the Mother of the Morning came because I was a reminder (merely a reminder) of a better mother (of my own mother's better *self*, the psychologist might explain today), why, then, *it was not my fault after all!* I did not have to accept a crippling guilt. The wickedness here rested altogether in the "stepmother," not the real mother; therefore, I could endure her mistaken criticisms of me; and I could love; I was set free to love completely and without fear; I needed only to wait till the Mother of the Evening reappeared—as surely she did, again and again throughout my childhood, for my mother *did* love me, and I was her son of a certainty.

Even so did I peer at the "real" world through the windows of a fairy tale. Even so did I find a certain fantastic sense in nonsense, and the sense preserved me. As I have indicated, this explanation is more subtle than I could think it through as a child. But that's the point: I didn't think it through. I lived it.

And I knew even then, on some functional level, that Snow White was "just" a fairy tale, and that I was engaged in a serious pretense. But the comfort it afforded me was actual. What the story *accomplishes* is as real as faith—or as the effects of psychiatric therapy. In those days I loved the better for it, walked the freer, *was* a better, healthier son and child.

Two: Lily, Entering the Story

The child," writes Bruno Bettelheim in *The Uses of Enchantment,* "is subject to desperate feelings of loneliness and isolation, and he often experiences mortal anxiety. More often than not, he is unable to express those feelings in words, or he can do so only by indirection."

Mortal anxiety: the sense of loss and endings. A suspicion of death. And then, surely, a cold encounter with death, when it enters the child's life as fact (whether suddenly or slowly, it doesn't matter). The wall against which life must crash . . .

It's my intent in the second half of this essay to anatomize the process by which children enter, stage by stage, the world which a fairy tale has woven for them—until, finally, the tale becomes their own most personal experience, reshaping (in this case) a mortal anxiety so that they *can* attend to it, to death, without being overwhelmed. The story must not deceive them! It cannot pretend there is no death where children have truly encountered death (as parents so often, in tenderness, try to do). But it can empower them.

In order to describe the general process of entering in, let me first present the particular context in which and for which *Lily* was created. It will give an illustrative substance to stages that must otherwise seem abstract.

On Tuesday the twenty-second of December, Miz Odessa Williams died of a cancer. She was elderly. Her own death was not untimely nor in other ways extraordinary—at least not to me, an adult and the pastor of the small congregation where she held membership. I had by then sat by many a bedside of the sick, stood by many a graveside of the dead.

On the other hand, as death itself is extraordinary to the living and the loving, and as *this* death was the first into which several children in our church had crashed heedless and headlong, it was to them scoundrel, monstrous, astounding.

My young daughter Mary, Dee Dee Lawrence, Herman Thomas, Timmy Moore, and three or four others had sung Christmas carols to her in the hospital just two days earlier. Miz Williams had responded with such frowning pleasure and praise, that the children had straightaway fallen in love with her. (I've written about that particular event elsewhere, the short story called "The Manger Is Empty" in the book *In the Days of the Angels.*) What a child loves, of course—especially when it is an older person—it becomes something like the polar star in that child's life. She orients herself by it. It is the very familiarity of her days.

But Odessa, fresh in the hearts of these children, died.

On Thursday morning at eleven o'clock we memorialized her with a funeral. The children attended. Before the service I accompanied my daughter Mary forward to the open casket, where the child gazed on the corpse, then touched Odessa's hand with the bare tip of her finger, then suddenly turned to me and burst into tears. Accusing tears. "It's Christmas Eve!" Mary cried, pressing her face into my stomach. "You're going to put Miz Williams in the ground on Christmas *Eve!*"

As quickly as she started, she stopped. My little daughter pinched her face, walked back to the pew where her mother was sitting, sat, folded her arms across her chest, and poked out her bottom lip.

She gave every sign of being angry.

So did Dee Dee. And Herman and Timmy.

During the service and the sermon that followed, others nodded and wept, dissolved, responded, made the moves of a gentle grief—walked with me the way of sorrow and healing.

But the children sat stuck, *un*-moving and unmoved. Angry, so it seemed to me, yet unexpressive of anger or of anything else.

Come the following Sunday, some of them were still continuing that shut-up behavior. I tried to talk with them, but they wouldn't respond with their true feelings, and I began to wonder whether there wasn't a streak of fear across their spirits. Anger in children can, by its surprising force, frighten them. But what if the anger is spontaneously turned against the greatest mysteries and the greatest authorities they know? The church. The pastor. God. What then? What retribution must follow *that* sort of insolence?

Well, so it occurred to me that the children were afraid to express their truer feelings, even to themselves, and that permission for this natural resentment should somehow be communicated to them.

Propositional language doesn't cut it, where children are concerned. It isn't enough to kneel before them (to kneel down as adults who are, after all, "ignorant" of the intensity of the fires within them) and to say, "It's okay. Go ahead and be angry."

Story, on the other hand, can ambush them. Story can walk them *without* retributive consequences to death and to rage and *through* the most sweet release of rage, to blessed conclusions—even before they have recognized exactly what in particular the tale is about.

So I made up the story now called "Lily."

On the following Sunday, in place of a formal sermon, I announced that I would be talking to the children, though adults could listen in if they wished. It was a simpler version I told them that day, but the elements were much the same as they are in this book.

When I said that Marigold thought of herself as a "knockout," they laughed. Oh, how dearly I had coveted that laughter, because it is precisely this, laughter, which proves the involvement of the *entire* child in the world the fairy tale is weaving around her: spirit and mind and body and lungs and humor. But more than involvement, laughter proves (permits) in them a sense of superiority over and against the evils which this story will confront. Laughter can be more than humor. Laughter can be a sharp gesture of contempt.

And when I said that the "Murderer" was coming, who could kill by kissing (an honest grotesquerie, as we cannot be *dis*honest with the images that must comprehend the deeper feelings of the child), I asked: "Who is the Murderer?"

Wonderfully, the children called out, "Winter!" though I had not given the name away. Yes, they were in it. Yes, it comported with the details of their daily experience.

But the whole purpose of the tale (as far as I was concerned on that particular Sunday) was to bring them to the point where they could, with Lily (with whom they identified, for all children consider themselves the youngest, the third, the most put-down), look death in the face and cry, "I hate you! I hate you!"

At that point in the tale I invited the cry.

And cry out they did: "I hate you, Murderer! I hate you, Death!"

I concluded the Lily story slightly differently then: I told the children that come *Easter* I could take them to that northern forest and I could show them the white blossom in which there trebled a waterdrop, which was no dewdrop, but the tear of life and love and gladness again.

It is, after all, central to our faith that we can hold death in vile contempt, freely and powerfully able to cross-examine it down to a maundering silence: "O death, where is your victory? O death, where is your sting?"

In fact, after a long career of telling children serious or silly stories, I am convinced that those who heard "Lily" that Sunday did not all enter it to the same depth, nor with the same personal intensity. Some went very deep. Some laughed, as it were, at the surface.

One of the most wholesome characteristics of the fairy tale is that each child can and will (albeit unconsciously) choose the level of reality at which he or she shall experience the tale. In other words, "Lily" can be mere fun on a Sunday morning, if that's all the child is prepared to experience at that point. Or, if the spirit of the child needs to and is emboldened to go deeper, "Lily" may be a personal, real encounter with death: at one level, death in general; at the deepest level, *this* death, the death of Odessa Williams. There is a natural safety factor in this form of communication, the fairy tale, fantasy, because it is the child's spirit that chooses the depth.

Roughly, I have found some six levels at which a child might experience a story like "Lily" or "Hansel and Grethel" or "Cinderella" or "Jack and the Beanstalk," and so forth. And one reason why children will ask for certain stories to be told over and over and *over,* is that they are dwelling within the place of the tale—and are moving deeper and deeper into it, as their spirits grow the more ready.

1. The story is a pleasant diversion. It isn't real. It is, in fact, a break from one's real life, like milk and cookies in the middle of the day, or like the twirl a father might give his little daughter, grabbing her hands and spinning her until they laugh together. It's an opportunity for companionship, for jokes and smiles, for a lightweight flight of imagination; but it's the fun that leaves the impression thereafter, not the tale itself.

2. The second level involves the child's admission of the general truth of the tale, that it has a sort of universal value: it is, she realizes, despite its fantastic elements, compatible with her own experiences. Yes, people are like this. Yes, these exaggerations are not just "made up." They represent things she has seen and felt and experienced abroad.

At this level she is paying attention to the story itself, not just to the teller and the fun of it all. On the other hand, she maintains a personal distance from its particularities (Hansel and Grethel's mother is *their* mother and in no way signals to the listening child her own or any mother she has ever met).

3. At the third level the child, conscious of her own selfness, perceives parallels between that self and the protagonist. There may be a mirroring quality to this relationship: the child remains the listener outside the tale, but at the same time "sisters" it with the child inside the tale, walks *with* her, as it were, but not yet with-*in* her. This is, surely, the beginning of identification. It is its own level of delightful, but earnest and concentrated "watching," as when children watch, say, fish in a tank, their spirits playing with the notion of seeing life through the fish's eyes, their mouths already making pop-pop-pop gestures.

But there still remains the film of separation between the listening child and the hero—and story still is story.

4. This is a transitional stage. When she is ready, she allows this stage to happen in an instant, whether at the first time she hears the tale, or at the thirteenth. *When she is ready:* she chooses. It is a discrete act accomplished by the child herself. Such is the proof of an emerging and independent personhood. And something like a living covenant is thereby established between herself and the story: what the story now becomes, it becomes at *her* volition.

What is the stage and the transition? The listening child releases her whole self into the tale. She enters the protagonist. Suddenly its setting, its populations, its narrative statutes and limits are altogether her world. And presently her personal history, her time—all the time of the outer world—spirals into the time and sequence of this world. This isn't so much the suspension of disbelief, as it is the present shape and behavior of all belief.

5. In consequence, the child assents to the particular experiential effects of this story. She wears the story like a glove, and now it becomes her own genuine experience.

The protagonist's actions are her actions. The words are her own, giving voice to notions and emotions she could not otherwise have uttered. As the narrative events flow, they bear her along like a chip in a river. The mothers *are* her mothers, the problems and the disasters are hers in the sufferance, even as the solutions (so often in fairy tales discovered within the protagonist, having lain there in secret all along) are likewise hers.

6. And sometimes the child's trust in the tale may go so far that she is no longer conscious of an external, listening, experiencing self. No longer does she "wear the story like a glove," as if there might yet be one degree of separation. The subject/object polarity (where once she was a subject reacting to, or else acting upon, the object of the story) is lost in perfect singularity. When the child utters word-for-word what the parent reads, she isn't speaking in unison with her parent or with the story, two voices *like* one; this is the *one* voice finding place in the child's own mouth.

Elements of her "real" life finally exist (and, for the story is duration, only exist) within the precincts of this tale.

The story is the temple, the child at devotions within it.

There is a remarkable passage in Deuteronomy 5:2-5, in which Moses utters a chronological impossibility as if it were the *only* possibility. To the children of Israel, about to cross the Jordan into the promised land; to Israelites who were born in the wilderness and who could therefore not have experienced in person the presence of God at the holy mountain in Horeb, Moses says: "The Lord our God made a covenant with us in Horeb." Now comes the comment that cannot be squared with mundane history: "Not with our fathers did the Lord make this covenant, but with us, who are all of us here alive this day. The Lord spoke with you face to face at the mountain, out of the midst of fire. . . ."

In Hebrew these words have a rhythmic, liturgical effect. They seem to have been recited over and over again down the ages by priests in celebration of the giving of the law, the Ten Commandments—which means that *often* those who could not have been physically at the mountain were told that, surely, they themselves had been at the mountain after all!

How do we interpret such an absurdity?

By recognizing the Hebrew's sense of sacred story. (Indeed, the sense that most oral cultures had regarding the telling of their epics, their myths and their histories.) When the story was being told, all time collapsed into *its* time; all time found purpose and meaning in *its* time; all human events received divine validation under *its* narrative events; a people experienced God again; and the past was thereby made present again— so that the hearers of the story were, truly, truly, there at the mountain, too.

No degree of separation.

No polarities.

Even so it may be for children crying out, "I hate you! I hate you, Death!"

Each one is speaking for herself and himself. *I* is each their "I." And *hate* is immediate hatred indeed. And Death is Death.

⁖

There was in my congregation at least one woman who remembered my stories and retold them when the times were right. Often I never wrote them down, feeling that they had served their purpose in the oral presentation. But Mary Ellen Phillips remembered. And Mary Ellen Phillips told them whenever she saw fit.

One day, nearly a year after I'd told "Lily" to the children, Mary Ellen came into my office with a tale of her own.

She had a niece, she told me, sixteen years old, the victim of a crippling disease. Rachel, who lived a great distance away from us, was confined to a wheelchair. In the course of several visitations, Mary Ellen had told Rachel the "Lily" story.

Recently Mary Ellen's sister had begged her please to come out for her daughter's sake. Rachel was grieving. She would neither eat nor speak with her family. She stayed in bed all day long, and the mother was at her wit's end.

Mary Ellen went, though she had no idea what she could do.

Rachel had loved a boy, also a teenager, also a quadriplegic, also bound to a wheelchair. One afternoon the boy's mother had wheeled him outside to take the air. She had parked the wheelchair on their back sidewalk facing away from the house, and had set the wheel lock.

But had not set it tight enough.

For after she had returned into the house, the chair began to roll downhill. It gathered speed. It hit a rut and slowly tipped over forward. This was the mildest of accidents. Yet when he landed facedown, something against the boy's windpipe shut off the air. And he suffocated to death.

This had been Rachel's beloved. His death was inexplicable. And horrid in her heart.

Mary Ellen told me that she arrived at her sister's house helpless, with no idea what to say or to do. She went into Rachel's bedroom. She sat down on Rachel's bed and looked at her. The child's lips were bitten and white.

But then it was Rachel herself who said, "Tell me 'Lily.'"

This request revived Mary Ellen. She had something to do, something to say to her niece. She told the tale all over again.

"Haw!" Rachel laughed with bitterness at Marigold. And "Haw!" at Bean Plant's pleading for life.

Later that same day, Rachel asked to hear "Lily" again.

And again.

Something within her needed the fairy tale, the way we sometimes crave salt, not understanding why.

But the child herself was not yet ready.

Until the next to the last day of Mary Ellen's visitation.

"Tell me 'Lily,'" Rachel demanded once more.

And this time, just as Bean Plant and Marigold were kissed by winter, Rachel burst into tears. She bowed her head and cried and cried. Finally, she had been ready to enter the story at the sixth level, personally and completely. And those deaths were not different—were in no way separate—from the death of her boyfriend.

Several years ago Mary Ellen Phillips hearkened back to that experience for me and added a postscript: that Rachel had since made the tale her own. That now she used it when others around her suffered the death of somebody dear.

When a story works, it becomes its own thing. It travels. It doesn't need its original author anymore.

But it *does* want a teller still.

And a child in need.

The Resurrection of Karen McDermott

Part One

nce upon a time there was a little girl—a very little girl, a miniature girl—who spent most of her days inside the pocket of her shirt.

Her name was *Shutup*.

Oh, yes, yes, indeed: little *Shutup* had a full-sized body, too. But this was a very big body, too big altogether: five feet tall in shoes, one hundred and fifty-six pounds of weight, a plain face, a huge mouth, and feet like rowboats. The full-sized Body could run, if the tiny girl forced it to run. And if she forced it to smile, it could smile exactly as if it were happy. Always the Body ate food on its own, without little *Shutup's* command; but the tinier girl could sometimes stop the Body, force it to sit with its hands in its lap and seem to be listening. "Seem," I say, because the big Body didn't really listen. Couldn't listen, really. And that's because the tiny girl wasn't listening either.

Now I must tell you a curious thing: *Shutup* did not use her full-sized body the way other people used theirs. The way you use yours. She didn't live in it. The tiny girl lived inside the pocket of the shirt that the big Body wore day after day. Like an enormous robot, the Body carried little *Shutup* here and there, back and forth, to school and to home and to her bedroom—which was her one and only private place in all the world.

Late at night when the Body undressed for bed, little *Shutup* would tell it to take her own tiny self out of the pocket and place her gently beside a jewelry box on the dresser. The Body would open the lid of that box and then go lie down on the bed and seem to sleep, exactly as other children *really* sleep.

The Body's first name was Karen. Its last name was McDermott, which was the same as the name of the tiny girl's mother, *Mrs.* McDermott.

While she stood on the dresser-top, little *Shutup* looked down at the gigantic Karen McDermott. She looked at the sad mouth, the plump cheeks, the straight unpretty hair. *Oh, me, oh, my,* thought *Shutup,* feeling sorry for the Body. She sighed and cried tiny diamond tears because the Karen-Body was so gross, so heavy and clumsy and ugly.

But immediately little *Shutup* frowned and scolded herself. *It's just a machine,* she said. *It doesn't have feelings. It's my robot. It's my . . . my royal carriage!* The Karen-Body was the puppet that took her place in the world so that no one would miss her or ask her difficult questions. Or laugh at *her,* at *Shutup.*

No sadness for Karen McDermott, then! No pity for a big machine.

Instead, little *Shutup* turned to the jewelry box with the lightness of a ballerina. She rose up on her toes and gazed into the mirror set in the open lid. *Ah, yes!* Her small heart jumped. *Oh, me! Oh, my!* Such a delicate face gazed back at her from the mirror: the mouth as small as a scratch in porcelain; the lips pale-pink and smiling; the cheeks as white as linen; and the two eyes brighter than ebony heads on silver pins.

Little *Shutup* stepped into the jewelry box. She crossed the field of red velvet, leaped onto the pedestal in front of the mirror—which now seemed like a stage in a theater—and she began to dance.

She danced to a tiny tinkling music in the clockwork of the box. She danced on the pedestal as it turned round and round. She lifted her right arm, slender and beautiful; and she, *Shutup,* became the grace of every swan in the world. She danced as the white swan swims, turning and turning the whole night through, never gross. Never gross was she, but ever steady and lovely.

But though the tiny child could dance an endless dance, there was one thing she could not do.

Shutup could not talk.

When morning came, the monstrous machine named Karen McDermott heaved itself out of bed and dressed and shuffled downstairs and made a huge breakfast and ate it.

Mrs. McDermott said to the sink, "I don't know why a twelve-year-old girl must eat like a lumberjack."

When it was done with breakfast, the great robot walked to school and sat down and seemed to listen.

The girl who sat behind the Karen McDermott Body had golden curls and sky-blue eyes. *Her* name was Claire Delaroche.

When Karen McDermott sat down, Claire Delaroche sang a little tune: "Fatty, fatty, where's your daddy?"

It's the same tune she had been singing every morning since September: *Fatty, fatty, where's your daddy?* Karen paid no mind to it.

But on this particular morning, Claire added a new verse to the tune. She stroked the back of Karen's head and sang sweetly, sweetly: "Fatty, fatty, two-by-four. Couldn't get through the kitchen door. Picked it up and did some more. No, that's not right," Claire said.

It didn't matter, of course. Nothing that Claire said could matter to Karen, because the big machine only *seemed* to listen.

Suddenly Claire yanked the Karen McDermott hair and hissed: "No! I should say, 'Turned around and *ate* some more,' right, Karen? Don't you eat three chickens a day? I can smell fry-grease in your hair."

No, no, no, no, no, no: nothing mattered to Karen the robot. And even if gross Karen happened by accident to listen; even if fat Karen happened to understand a word or two, that didn't matter either, because this is the truth about robots and machines: they don't have feelings. They can't feel anything at all.

Part Two

ere is how *Shutup* learned that her name was *Shutup*. . . .

Last year, before she had moved out of the Body called Karen McDermott, her mother said, "This is not my child." Over and over Mrs. McDermott repeated the same declaration in different words: "*My* child would never do something like this."

Do something like what?

Like cry.

During that year Karen had cried and cried. She couldn't help it. Exactly like a two-year-old she bawled and dribbled and drooled. Karen cried messy and headlong and loud.

Not my child! My daughter would never do this.

And why was she crying?

Well, it began when her daddy walked away, leaving Karen and Mrs. McDermott in the house alone.

He didn't come back at the end of the day, or the end of the week, and Karen began to sniffle and whimper. She missed him. But Mrs. McDermott said nothing about the man who had left, who was Karen's father. She only said, "This is not my child."

Her daddy had left with nothing but his satchel-bag.

Karen had said to him, "What's in your bag?"

He laughed and said, "My underpants."

She laughed, too. "How come your underpants?" she said.

"A man must have clean underpants," he said, "when he travels the wide, wide world."

He tickled her ribs and she giggled: "Hee hee." They were in Karen's bedroom, where had had stopped before leaving.

But suddenly he was hugging her so tight that it hurt her ribs.

"Little girl, this is for you," he said. He reached into his satchel-bag and pulled out a jewelry box of polished ebony. With great care he placed the box on the top of her dresser. He opened the lid. A tiny ballerina popped up; a tiny music began to play; and the ballerina turned round and round and round. Karen's heart almost stopped at the beauty before her, and the love of the daddy that gave it to her.

When the clockwork wound down and the music stopped; when she looked around to thank her daddy, she saw that he and his satchel were gone. Gone from the bedroom. Gone from the house.

He didn't come back at the end of the month. By that time Karen was whining a scared sort of whine.

"When is daddy coming home?" she asked her mother.

And Mrs. McDermott answered with one word, as if she were very angry. "Never," she said.

Never? How could it be *never?*

On that night, then, Karen began to cry out loud. She stuffed her face into her pillow so that her mother shouldn't hear her, but she cried like a two-year-old: "Boo-hoo! Boo-hoo!" until she fell asleep.

Along about midnight she woke up because she heard somebody pounding something somewhere in the house.

She got up and followed the sound. It was in the kitchen. It was her mother, with two fists pounding on the kitchen table. "I'm tired, I'm tired," her mother was whispering to herself. "It's not my fault. I don't deserve such pain and torment," she hissed like a woman broken at the throat.

Torment? Why, it had not occurred to Karen that her mother was as sad as she was herself.

It was after her mother had gone to bed and after she had fallen asleep, that Karen figured out how to comfort her poor mother. She got up and went on bare feet into her mother's bedroom. She crawled under the covers beside Mrs. McDermott and began to pat her back.

Softly she said, "It's okay, Mama. Everything will be all right."

Suddenly the woman screamed, *Yow!* and flew out of bed. "McDermott! McDermott!" she yelled.

This is what she used to call Karen's daddy when she was mad at him: McDermott. It's how she scolded him when he was naughty.

"No, Mama!" Karen cried. "No, it's *me!*"

Her mother ran to the doorway and flipped on the light. "You?" she snapped. "Who said *you* could come in here? Why did you want to scare me so? Get out! Get out!"

Karen began to cry. Slowly she began to climb out of the bed, waiting for her mother to change her mind. But instead of changing her mind, Mrs. McDermott grabbed her daughter's arm and yanked her to the door and pushed her through it and then slammed it in Karen's face.

Karen McDermott leaned her forehead against the door. She cried louder and louder. She slid down to the floor, howling with great sadness.

But even as loud as she was crying, her mother was louder, shrieking inside her bedroom: "Shut up! Shut up! Shut up! Shut up! You aren't my daughter. *Shut up!*"

So that is how the days and the nights went thereafter. Karen's mother would not talk to her. So Karen couldn't help it: she cried. *Then* her mother would talk, but she would only say the same things over and over: "This is not my daughter. Shut up, please. Shut up."

Finally, when Karen was crying in the middle of the night, Mrs. McDermott came out of her bedroom and rushed into Karen's bedroom. "I told you 'Shut up,'" she said. Her eyes were twitching left and right, looking for something. They found the ebony jewelry box on the dresser. "I told you," she said, "now I'll *make* you shut up."

I'll make you Shutup.

Mrs. McDermott went to the dresser. She opened the jewelry box. The tiny ballerina popped up. The tiny music began to play. But this time the ballerina did not turn around. Mrs. McDermott, hissing the words, "Your father was a wastrel!" reached for the pretty ballerina and, *Snap!*—broke it from the pedestal. She shook it at Karen. She threw it down on Karen's bed. "Shutup, Shutup, Shutup," she hissed, then she left the bedroom and slammed the door.

And here is an amazing thing: it worked. Karen *did* shut up. It surprised even her that suddenly she wasn't crying any more. But neither did she sleep.

The very next day at school another thing happened almost exactly like the thing that had happened the night before.

While the teacher was reading a story to the whole class, Claire Delaroche, who sat *beside* Karen McDermott that year, passed a note to Karen. The words on the note were printed in big, thick letters, on account of Claire's sky-blue eyes: they were near-sighted. They couldn't see things clearly. But the beautiful Claire refused to wear glasses.

So the huge letters spelled:

KAREN MAC DERMIT

DRINGS FROM THE TOILET

HER DADDY . . .

But that's as far as Karen could read the note. As soon as she saw the word "DADDY," she started all over again to cry. She opened her mouth wide and she howled and dribbled and drooled.

The teacher looked up. The teacher stamped her foot and said, "Oh, shut up! Why can't you be like the other children? Shut up! Shut up!"

In that very instant, the girl obeyed. And she changed—changed everything without even thinking about it.

She did, indeed, "shut up." She shut up Karen McDermott's big mouth, so there was no crying any more, no noise at all. She shut up Karen McDermott's whole Body: shut up the windows and all the doors, as if that Body were a house for sale; then she her-self—a tiny, pretty girl—moved out of the Body and into the shirt pocket, never to utter another word, never ever again.

She left the name "Karen McDermott" for the monstrous machine, for the mechan-ical robot that everyone else (all the adults and all the children) called "Karen McDermott." And she knew her own truer name, because this is what they called *her,* the real girl that used to live inside gross Karen McDermott. The real girl's name was *Shutup,* and *Shutup* is what they made her. *Shutup* is what she became.

And now she thought she was happy. No one could find her any more. No more teasing. No more scolding. No more crying. No more troubles. No more talking. The miniature girl with the porcelain mouth—she planned to stay silent forever.

Part Three

"Fatty, fatty, where's your daddy?"

The reason why Claire Delaroche knew so much about the life of Karen McDermott is that the McDermotts and the Delaroches were neighbors. When they were little girls they used to play together. In those days there wasn't even a fence between their yards. When they went to kindergarten they held hands because they were best friends, and both were a little scared to be going away from home. They sat beside each other on the school bus.

And even though Karen would sometimes cry when she was little, it didn't matter to Claire, because she cried sometimes, too. It's what children did when they were scared. And they relieved the fear by crying *together*.

And Karen knew that Claire could hear it when her own mother and father screamed at each other. It's why Claire didn't ask why Karen was crying sometimes in the morning. But Karen knew that her best friend understood, because she took her hand. They waited for the bus holding hands together.

But somewhere between the third grade and the fifth grade things changed.

Karen McDermott grew bigger and bigger on account of her eating. She still cried, though. Every first day after every vacation from school she felt so terribly homesick, that she would put her head down into her arms on the desk and boo-hoo so loud that the other children whispered. They giggled. And Claire Delaroche stayed away from her at recess then. And after school, Claire would sit by somebody else on the bus.

One afternoon in the fourth grade, Karen got off the bus and went into her house and found that it was empty—no mother there, no father, just herself alone. Someone had polished all their hardwood floors. Someone had moved all the furniture into other rooms. The wax smell was everywhere, and the sound of the whole house was as hollow as a cave. Karen burst into tears. She wailed and wailed because she thought that her parents had moved away without telling her about it. She rushed next door to Claire's house, still drooling and dribbling and howling out loud. But when Claire opened her door, she whispered, "Go away. You shouldn't come over without asking."

Karen heard giggling inside Claire's house. That's why Claire was whispering. She had some girlfriends with her. Maybe it was a party.

Claire whispered, "You look ugly when you cry." And she shut the door.

And here was another change during those years: while Karen was just growing big, Claire Delaroche was growing into a knockout. She was beautiful: bright, sky-blue and squinting eyes; a golden fall of hair, all ringlets and the softest waves. She had learned a certain kind of giggling—a sort of "Look-at-me" giggling, a "See-how-I-don't-care-about-a-thing" giggling—which made the other girls fall all over themselves to become her friend. To get invited to her house.

And Karen had a suspicion that *another* way which Claire had for getting the girls on her side was to make fun:

Fatty, fatty, Cincinnati. . . .

Who would mock the girl who mocks better than anyone?

And maybe Claire was proving to everyone that she and Karen McDermott had *never* been friends, or surely not the best of friends:

Fatty, fatty, Cincinatti,
Face is snotty, hair is nappy. . . .

By the time they were eleven years old Karen McDermott always sat alone in the front seat of the school bus. Claire sat with a whole flock of pretty girls in the back.

"Do you know," she sang aloud, giggling, "what Fatty McDermott wants to be when she grows up?"

Luckily, this was on the same day when little *Shutup,* the tiny child, had moved out of the gross Karen-Body and into the pocket of its shirt. Luckily, I say, because today the Karen-robot was only seeming to listen, and all her feelings were gone. She didn't feel anything.

"Well, I'll tell you," Claire Delaroche giggled and giggled: "A dancer! Can you believe that? A *dancer!*"

Never mind. Never mind.

It didn't matter.

Because in silence and in private, indeed, indeed, this very night, the miniature girl will cross a field of blood-red velvet and step up on a pedestal and gaze into the glass before her, where she will see a delicate figure whose mouth is as small as a nick in porcelain, whose cheeks are whiter than linen, whose eyes are black as the ebony heads of little pins—and she will dance.

She *will* dance.

Part Four

ut they were twelve, now. Twelve years old. And Claire sat behind the mechanical robot, Karen McDermott, in the sixth grade class at school. And that big Body never turned around, no matter how hard Claire tried to get its attention. No feelings or wounds or hurts at all. Safe. A fortress for little *Shutup*, hidden in its pocket.

Safe, yes. But finally not safe enough.

Every fortress has a door, and every hiding place a hole.

And sometimes, in a single instant, all the walls fall down, and there we are, blinking in the sunlight, unhidden, and *there!*

This is what happened:

Home the children were going in the school bus, the gross Karen in the front seat of the bus, taking up two spaces, sitting alone; and the beautiful Claire surrounded by giggling girls in the back.

Home they were going on a warm spring day. No one was singing tunes about Karen. Maybe the Body was actually disappearing from view. Could that be possible? The bus windows were open. The breezes came in. There were yellow jonquils and handsome daffodils bursting in the yards of the neighborhoods.

Home they came to the street where the McDermott and the Delaroche houses sat side-by-side with a fence between them; and here the bus pulled to a stop across the street, in the exact same spot where it had stopped for six years now.

The mechanical Body called Karen rose up and descended the steps and went out on the sidewalk. It walked around to the front of the bus and began to cross the street.

Claire would be coming behind, though Claire would wait a while, allowing the Karen-Body to go first and alone.

Just as the Karen-Body was about to step up on the far side of the curb, it heard a sound and it paused. Actually, *Shutup* must have heard the sound, too. They both paused. They both turned and looked up the road, the way the bus had come.

A purple car was driving this way, very fast, not slowing down.

Why wasn't it slowing down? Maybe it thought that this Karen was the only Body to be crossing the street, that there were no more students to come.

No more students?

Yes! One more student!

Karen and *Shutup* turned further to look behind them, and there she was! Claire, coming 'round the bus.

Karen screamed, "Claire! Look out!"

But the beautiful girl wasn't wearing her glasses, squinting and squinting, and coming still, into the path of the purple car.

And then Karen didn't think. She acted. She ran back across the street as fast as she could and jumped to push Claire out of the way. And she did: she knocked Claire out of the way, but her own backside got hit by the purple car, and she flew through the air for about six feet before she skidded to a stop, but she had kept her eyes on Claire all the while, to make sure that her friend wasn't hurt.

Claire wasn't hurt.

Karen was hurt. The Body had taken a real bump, and felt it. She would soon be bruised all over her rear end. But more important than that, she had felt fear for Claire! And she had felt the memory of friendship for Claire. She had feelings!

And more important even than *that: Shutup* had talked!

She had said, "Claire. Look out."

She wasn't shut up any more.

She was right there, back inside the body of Karen McDermott, out in the open once more.

And this was the proof: Claire Delaroche was looking at her. At *her!* And on Claire's face was the very same look of fear that Karen had felt on her own face before. And maybe some of that fear was for her, for Karen, still sitting bruised on the ground in front of the bus.

And then this is what happened next: even before the driver of the purple car had jumped out and run back to the two girls, Claire knelt down beside Karen, and she took her hand, and both of them began to cry—not diamonds, but real tears warm and wet.

They sat in the street and cried together, exactly as friends do.

So that's how Karen became Karen again.

Wish

O Wind, I watch how you dance with the branches,
Laugh in the green leaves, whirl in the tree—
O Wind, I raise my arms and I whisper,
　　Dance with me.

O mighty West Wind, driving the white clouds
Over the blue sky like ships on the sea—
O sailing Wind, is there, on your sky-ship,
　　Room for me?

O roaring storm-Wind, flashing lightning,
Spitting rain like an enemy—
Don't hate me. There are already too many
　　Mad at me.

Dear Wind, come lift me like a dry leaf,
Spin me to heaven; I'm not afraid.
Allow me, Wind, to fly on your long breath
　　Far away.

The Shaper

Part One: Forged in Relationship

When our children were young it was my custom to tell them stories in the dark, in their bedrooms, in the tender dreamish warmth before they fell asleep. I sat in a chair tipped back on its hind legs. The children lay tucked beneath their covers. I smoked. I have since quit; but in those days I, the tale-teller and their father, smoked a pipe whose aroma (I hoped) would ever thereafter attend their memories of—could possibly even *trigger* their memories of—those holy, communal moments and the murmurous music of my voice.

I made the stories up, most often right there on the spot.

I shaped the stories to fit their days and each their individual personalities. Every child became the hero of his and her own story—though the names were changed and the settings were mostly at some safe distance from the grit world around us.

For an entire season, once, I raveled out in nighttime episodes a longish tale about Orphay and Dice. It was loosely based on the myth of Orpheus, whose beloved Eurydice had descended into the underworld, Hades, the land of the dead, after being fatally wounded by a snake. There the King of the Dead, also named Hades, ruled with his queen, Persephone. Orpheus, who was imputed to have introduced music to the world, the sweetness of whose music could turn a dead tree green again, begged to descend into Hades in order to bring his beloved up to sunlight and life again. Orpheus played music so sweet, the whole of the underworld was moved—even cold-hearted Hades. "Yes," said Hades. "she may go with you—but only so long as you do not turn to see if she is following!" And the treachery of so seeming-easy a task is, of course, that Eurydice made no sound in the following. Orpheus had no evidence she was there. He had to proceed on blind faith and faith alone. . . .

In my version, Orphay and Dice were much younger than in the myth; and rather than Greek, they were African American, as was the whole culture around us; yet Orphay's power remained in his music, the drumming, the sound and the subtle rap. For though his brother Matthew was our black son and he our white, it was Joseph who was the artist, after all, filled with subtlety and sensitivity and remarkable music. This, therefore, was Joseph's story, his naming, and the early enunciation of his purpose in life.

Today he is a sculptor, still the artist whom I had shaped by story.

But I never wrote that story down.

Sometimes I would, as it were, toss a story out to all the children, just tell the tale until it found its ending (for it is usually the story that takes me along for the ride rather than I the story). If none of the four children asked to hear it again, then that was the end of its life. The tale had served its purpose, and then had passed away. There was no sorrow nor any loss in that: stories take up their existence always in relationship. It is the relationship that endures, affected deeply or lightly by the tale, which is its servant. The effect remains as a characteristic of the relationship. (It cannot be the other way around, that relationships serve an artist's art, a writer's craft, for then the writer has begun to worship his talent and his vocation, and his art can become the god that consumes the people around him. This is dangerous and destructive.)

On the other hand, one of the children might ask to hear that story again. And again. And then I knew that she had made it her own: it nursed some internal hunger within her; and with every telling the story was reshaped not just by my creativity, but also by my child's tiny responses, sighs, gestures, words, dialogues, demands, requests, exclamations, giggles, refusals. For this is the way it has always been with the best of storytellers: what they utter is also forged in relationship. The thing is born and reborn in community. It is the moves of an intricate dance, requiring the tale-teller to be as alert to his audience as he is to his material.

In this way, for example, the story now published as *In the Beginning There Was No Sky* actually became my daughter's story, chosen by her and then shaped in the living nexus of our relationship, in our mutual love and trust. Only when she was done with it, her need of it having passed away; only when she and *No Sky* had detached from one another, did I tell it to others (to adults, in fact) and discover in their strong emotional responses how universal was the particular need of my daughter. Then, therefore, on account of the mute assent of the broader community, I chose to write the story down and offer it in print to the public. And though I cannot know the many who have read it since, it is my conviction that by means of this story we have, writer and readers, compacted together an enduring relationship: spiritual, if not physical; in the fictive place and time of the tale itself, if not in the fiercely fixed dimensions of "real" time and space.

Often the seed of an evening story came from the children themselves, some childish metaphor they may have used during the day, which I would then have taken seriously and permitted to become the controlling image of the entire story. In that case I became for them not much more than a sophisticated mirror, reflecting in large the thought they had produced in small and in a flash.

For example, Talitha, the youngest of our children, once said to me: "Daddy, your work eats you up, doesn't it?"

I was a pastor in those days. I was good. I mean, as a pastor I *had* to be good the day long; but by the time I came home, I was often wearied by my well-doing—and no longer good. I griped. I was impatient. I could utter thunder in my judgments. And I, like the storm, could chase my children inside—inside themselves, away from me.

But Talitha explained it, by the indirection of her metaphor, much in my favor: ministry consumed me. *Your work eats you up.*

Now, rather than peer *through* the metaphor to some simple, propositional interpretation of it (which must, finally, diminish all that is implied in such a rich figure of speech) the storyteller accepts it as is; blows a fuller life into it, so that it becomes not a single figure but an entire fantasy; and allows it to represent (in the experience of story) much more than his poor discursive mind could ever comprehend on its own.

I turned it into a story.

I allowed the major character to manifest characteristics of Talitha herself. She cried much when we first adopted her. And her tears embarrassed her, drew the mockery of her three siblings. But her tears, I sincerely believed, were born as well of tenderness (not only of vulnerability, but also of a watchful sympathy).

So the story was about a potato farmer and his wife, who had four children: Pine, the oldest and full of pride as a problem-solver; Oak, all full of pride in his physical aptitude; Rose, all full of pride in her beauty (in succession recognizable as Joseph, Matthew, and Mary); and Thistle, who cried all the time, at which her siblings sneered, "Oh, Thistle, can you do nothing but cry? No, nothing but cry."

Near the beginning of the story, the farmer uncovers a potato twice as big as he is himself, whose thousand eyes, one by one, pop open!

The potato begins to talk.

"My name is Pudge!" it roars. "I'm hungry! I'm hungry and ready to eat! And here is my dinner before me. Man, I'm going to eat *you!*"

Which is exactly what the potato does: eats the potato farmer, "shoes, shovel and all."

Grim? Indeed. But not grimmer than my daughter's metaphor—and fantastic enough that it remains a figure at several removes from "real" life.

As the story continues, Pudge swallows down, one by one, the whole family, till Thistle is left alone. And crying. But those tears become the salvation of the whole family, because her kindness allows an old crone to kiss them, at which each tear becomes a thorn—and when Pudge swallows *her* down, she sticks and stabs his gullet until he bursts open and the whole family emerges, now dancing gladness around the youngest child of all, Thistle—for they have been saved by her love, saved from their father's work, which had eaten everyone else up.

Now, this is the same method I followed in the development of the story that precedes this essay: "The Resurrection of Karen McDermott." Its formative process is something of a reversal upon the method used for "Lily." In "Lily" the author makes up the controlling metaphor and offers it to the children in service of their need. In "Thistle" and in "Karen McDermott," however, the author finds the controlling metaphor already in use by the child, where it is already accomplishing a highly complex service for the child. (Karen affects indifference by investing her more sensitive self in a secret and separate object, as other children place their truest attentions, their fundamental loyalties in, say, a hobby, or a hidden and protected place, a pet, some self-affirming fantasy.) The author's job, then, is merely to give that metaphor latitude and sequence, space and time, for larger growth and a deeper investigation. As long as the metaphor remains intact—*not* analyzed, *not* interpreted, but only expanded—it continues to serve and to nurse in ways beyond the storyteller's capacity ever to comprehend. (Ever and ever, our stories should be smarter than we are, or else they might as well be lessons, teachments, preachments, instructions limited to our poor intellects.)

By this method, once more, the story is born in the relationship between a watchful artist and his watching audience.

It is an intense communion.

And I, as a storyteller, am for my child, for my congregation, for my community, for the public at large . . . I am the Shaper.

Part Two: Story and History, Shaping the Day

uring the Renaissance, poets delighted in the Greek sense of the word *poet*. Ben Jonson (in *Timbers*) defines it as "the maker." The poet was perceived as a creator not unlike the Primeval Creator of All.

But I personally find its older, Sanskrit meaning much more congenial to the task I think I do. The Sanskrit cognate, *cinoti,* makes of the poet "a heaper into heaps, and a piler into piles."

We artists, we writers—we come upon the stuff of our crafty attentions already there. But we find it a mess. Hopeless. A meaningless chaos. Our job is to organize. To order. To heap certain things with certain things over here, and to pile other things over there. To declare associations and differences and relationships. To make of this chaos a cosmos, which we do by translating things into language, and language into character and episode, and episodes into whole stories. Under our craft, time is no longer a series of endlessly repeated *ticks.* For every tick we offer a *tock.* For every beginning, a palpable and satisfying end. An "end," that is, a purpose, a value, a "point to which" all these piled-up things do tend, and in which they may be fulfilled.

Our poems *are* that order. Our songs and our stories do more than persuade others that an order exists: they build the house; they weave a world; they companion our listeners *into* the experience of such ordered cosmos.

Another ancient word: the Old English word which is translated as *poet* today, is *Scop.* It's pronounced "shop." And it is the ancestor of our present word: *Shape.*

Our forebears knew that the task of the minstrel, of the community's tale-telling singer, was to sing amorphous, overwhelming events into shape.

Let's say, for example, that a seventh century community has just fought a day's battle with their nearest enemy. Hand-to-hand they fought until the dark descended with forces more frightening than any human could be. The battle had been bloody enough to make a red mud of the earth beneath their feet; and one of their number had died; and now they've returned to the mead hall, exhausted, hungry, aggrieved.

They eat in silence. They drink that oldest of human drinks, a wine made of fermented honey. Their sadness deepens to a maudlin despair. . . .

And just then the singer strikes a chord on his harp.

Everyone listens.

The singer develops the chord into melody. A familiar melody, in fact. One everyone has heard since childhood, and therefore one that carries profound, unutterable associations: parental comfort, an assurance of the divine. The singer sings familiar verses, and all the people nod: there is the weight of meaning in these verses. They remember. They remember and reexperience them now.

But then the singer begins to weave new words into the familiar verses: the details of today's grim battle; the name of the comrade who fell; the deeds he did in falling, all of which, fetching up in the experience of this song, find place within the precincts of the divine; all of which are no longer senseless, but do bear now the weight of genuine purpose and meaning. And the people nod. And the dead ascends into the Valhalla of heroes. It is well. Chaos is cosmos. Desolation is now heavy with purpose. The day has taken shape in the singer's song—

—and ever thereafter, it is the spiritual, artistic shape which is remembered as the truth of that day, not the cold, undecipherable, purely empirical fact.

In my day and in my experience as the singer, the song I might sing is the twenty-third psalm. And the story I tell will always, always have a narrative familiarity to my wounded listeners; its pattern is ever the same. But the details will invite their particular sorrows, their particular persons and histories, to enter the tale anew. And the power of the old, old story will prop them up in all their leaning places.

The poet withdraws for the sake of the story.

And the story exists for the sake of relationship.

Saxifrage, the Break-Rock

Part One

nce upon a time there was a child who did nothing but sit by her window and sigh. She believed that as long as she lived she could never open her mouth again. So she didn't.

Sometimes her daddy would slip into the room and tell her some interesting bit of business and then smile. But she wouldn't smile back at him. Maybe he would ask her a question about her day, but she wouldn't answer. She never opened her mouth. She was afraid that if she did, she might hurt him.

Of all the children in the world, she was the most beautiful. Her eyes were a haze at sunset. Her face was a loaf of bread come soft from the oven, smoky gold and so plump it broke her daddy's heart to look at her—because of all the children in the world, she was the saddest, too.

So he slipped from the room again in silence, sadly.

And the little girl would do what she always did, would stare through her window at the ragged streets of the city and sigh. There was a secret inside the child so dreadful that no one should ever discover it, a devil so dangerous no one should ever see. That's why she kept her mouth closed.

Now, it happened that a young man began to parade down the girl's street, right by her window.

"Melons!" he cried—but he pronounced it "Mee-loans!" and he was selling them. "Hey! Great round mee-loans for great round bellies! Mee-loans sweet, for sweeter hearts!"

The little girl stared at him, but she gave him no expression, and perhaps he took that for a challenge. For he came back daily, every day. And every day he came back livelier than the day before.

"Whoop! I got me a load o' sweet fat cawn! Green jackets an' a yallow skin! Strip 'em bare, and bite right in!" He was always pushing a grocery cart full of goods, extolling his goods in shameless phrases—extolling himself, don't you know. A scam-man, folks might say. A jive salesman selling anything under the sun. A skinny whip of a hawker, tireless and happy, outrageously happy for these dreary streets.

"*Greens* all bitter to a black man's tongue!" he shouted, clapping his hands at his own fine rap. "Whoop! Greens to remember the hickory switches an' yo' ol' black mama, yeah!" The scam-man sent a distinct wink to the girl in the window, then roared on down the street: "Buy collard greens in honor of yo' mamas, yeah!"

So one day it was melons, another corn, another greens. And then he came with fish he said he caught himself. And candles, crying, "I *am* the light!" And sometimes he gave it out that he was sharpening knives. And the scam-man danced in the middle of the street, and he shouted and sang and popped his lips and winked at the girl in the window. And inevitably, he drove his cart by a round route to the window itself, so that one day he snatched his hat from his head and made a low bow right in front of the child who watched him. He swooped his arm around himself like an actor of fame, peeped up at her, winked once more, then shuffled backward, butt-first, shaking in merriment, all full of himself, thoroughly impressed by his own theatrical ways.

The little girl stared. Who wouldn't? But she did not smile. She did not open her mouth. Yet something, when she saw that low bow, twitched deep inside of her. Perhaps it was gladness. Maybe just interest. It made her a tiny bit sorrier.

And so it went as the weeks went by.

The scam-man sang a signifying tune, strutting while he sang it, declaring his hand-someness (though he was bone-thin), his street-wise sass (though she never noticed that he made a sale), his inborn talents (though his tune was more raucous than melo-dious, more shout than song). He cut a ridiculous figure, tall and grand and skinny as a flagpole. And all this would have been fine with her, the daily diversion would have been pleasant to her, except that finally he did something terrible and wonderful at once, and the poor girl began to worry. Worse, she began to fear. The scam-man spoke directly to *her*.

"Hey, girl!" he cried suddenly, as though just noticing her. "Hey, you pretty pack o' somethin' in yo' winda!" he shouted, sashaying toward her building, then stutter-stepping back again. He was shouting and dancing at once. "Why you never smile at me?" Oh, her tummy tightened then; he was talking to her, and he was talking *about* her, causing her to notice herself. "Where you get the strength to fight my charms? Whoop! I'm a flat-down, jump-up strap of a beautiful boy, I am. The bes' o' the breed," he cried. "Then how you able to resist my irresistible style?"

He fired the questions at her, but he never waited for an answer, always twirling off as though stunned by the questions themselves, the marvelous mind in his own head.

The poor girl gazed at him. It was a low window; she was only slightly higher than his bony frame when he came close; but someone might have called her haughty anyway, as though she were watching from a high, embattled tower, because she never opened her mouth or smiled or broke her scowl or did any such thing.

"'S-okay! 'S-okay!" the scam-man declared. "'S-awright! One day I whittle you down, woody girl. But for today, I got m'things to sell, m'money to make, an' corporate business deals to transact. Bye, you pretty pack o' somethin'. Bye, an' I be back."

Then he and his cart and the show and the noise all clattered on down the street and away.

But the poor girl sat in her window and suffered. Things had changed. Because, for the first time since she had shut her mouth forever, this outrageous fool had made her want to laugh. *Flat-down, jump-up strap of a beautiful boy,* he had said, and her stomach had squeezed with laughter, delighted. You can't control your stomach. But you can fight it, and she did. By a mighty act of will, the sad child had commanded the laugh to stay in her stomach, where it became a dead lump of simple pain, and the pain—it felt like sorrow. So now she wanted to cry. But she didn't do that either.

She could not, and she would not, open her mouth for anything, not for laughter, not for tears. If she so much as smiled, her secret would show, and then even the happy salesman would be horrified by the evilness inside of her, and he would run away with loathing, and that would be just one more person whom she liked, but whom she killed.

So she kept her mouth shut soberly, and nothing in her face. No, nothing at all, save sadness.

Part Two

 or this was the poor girl's secret: that she had no tongue in her mouth as other people do. Instead, there was a snake.

Now, a snake in your mouth can be a shocking, frightfully ugly thing.

But in her case it was worse than that. This snake could kill by a bite of poison. And whom did it kill especially? The people she loved. So the only way to handle such a snake is to keep it shut behind your teeth. Never, never open your mouth, or the snake will fly out and strike.

Twice when the child had opened her mouth to people she loved, the serpent-tongue had struck. Twice it had turned them to cold stone. It should never happen again. She'd learned her lesson. Never talk again.

So now you know why she sits so sadly in her window. And now you know why she cannot laugh for the scam-man. She is not haughty. She is dangerous.

For the first one that she turned to stone was her mother, but then she wasn't sure that she had done it. She only had suspicions.

But the second one that she turned to stone was her brother, and that was the proof, because she saw the snake fly out.

This is how it happened:

After their mother died (while still the girl could not prove it was her fault) she loved her brother more than ever. Their daddy was distant then. He worked the second shift, and when he was home he walked through the whole house groaning. So the little girl told her brother: "June, I will love you." And she thought of a way to say that they needed each other now more than anything. She said: "June, I will love you just like mama."

Just like mama.

And she did. She kept her word. She loved her brother every minute of the day, desperately.

But after their mother died, the boy, who was seven years older than she, began to change. And they began, therefore, to argue. And the more she loved him, the more they argued. So loving grew harder and harder inside of her.

In the evening she said, "Why you quit goin' to school, June?"

He was brushing and brushing his hair in front of a mirror. He stopped and said, "How you know that?"

She said, "Don' matter how, June. What matters is, where you get them lizard-skin shoes? Where you get yo' pleated pants?"

Nasty and uppity at once, he said, "Ain' none o' yo' bid-ness!"

"*You* my business, June," she said. "You my brother. What you doin' in the daytime now? What you doin' in the night that shames you so?"

"Shuddup!" he said, brushing his hair the harder.

But she said, "Where you get your money now?"

And then he turned on her.

Her brother was always a wizard with words. He could make the language work for him, could talk himself into anything or out of anything. So now he aimed that language straight at his sister with no remorse, because he was changing.

"Licorice stick!" he called her, squinting one eye and pointing his finger like a gun. "Domino! Peppercorn! Dirt! Charcoal brick, not a spark o' sense in yo' coal-black haid!" So she felt that the love was writhing inside of her. "Girl, you tar in a world that likes milk better! A sticky mess I step in it," he snapped. It was getting worse and worse. "You slow me down, y'hear?" And then he told her he was wiping her from his shoe, and he strutted out the door, and he slammed it.

So the love got harder and harder inside of her. It felt like a thick thing in her throat, something she couldn't swallow down. It felt like a rope coiled in her breast, tight and terrible and evil, though she didn't understand how love could be evil. It made her tremble.

And then one night her brother came home, leering with liquor. She could smell it. He stood in her doorway and roused her up by shouting about the worldly things he had done that night, things that she would never do, and therefore they were different, he said. Completely different. He was laughing nasty. And the more he laughed, the thicker grew the love in her throat. Huge: it blocked her breathing. Huge: it swelled like a vomit, and she thought that she was suffocating.

But then he said one thing too many, and suddenly the love burst out on its own. She opened her mouth and screamed at her brother. She screamed about the grief of their dead mama, and the bite in her scream was that she called him, called June, a wicked, vile, cruel name, the worst she'd ever heard of to use—

No! No, but she didn't scream at all. Something different happened, a monstrous, terrifying thing: the love that shot from her mouth, it was a snake, a long thick snake, a savage hissing snake! It lunged up from her stomach and straight to her brother's face, and it bit him like hatred, though it was love—and she saw it!

She gasped, and she sucked it back inside herself. Too late! Her brother was stunned. Her brother was frozen to absolute silence. Her brother stood in the doorway like stone. Stone.

Then neither she nor her brother spoke. She was scared to speak. And he, as she saw, could not speak. Cold and stony went his face, paralyzed (yes! yes!) by the poison. Day to day he was a walking statue, like the carving in the cemetery. It used to be that the boy could talk himself out of anything. But two nights later the police came and picked him off the street like picking a berry from a bush, and he said nothing to save himself, no, nothing at all. So they put him in some kind of hospital prison, where he lay on his back and stared at the ceiling as good as dead.

And the poor girl knew that she had done it. Nobody but her.

And now she had the proof, and now she knew one other terrible thing as well. That she was the one that turned their mama into stone.

For their mama had been sick for many months, and the little girl (she admitted this now) had grown tired of bringing her mama water; the little girl (she remembered this so clearly now) had been mad that her mama wasn't getting well and getting up. In fact, the little girl let herself think that her mama should *quit*—should be *done* with diseases and sicknesses and everything. Just quit and be done.

With all these feelings inside of her, the little girl had whispered in her mama's ear one night: "I love you, Mama. I wished you would sleep. I wished you would sleep the deepest sleep ever."

Oh, poor, sad, miserable child! *The deepest sleep ever:* she got her wish.

On the following morning she had found her mother cold in bed, all stony on the pillow, a dusty statue of her living self.

And now that she had actually seen the snake that stunned her brother, well, she knew exactly what had happened to her mother. *I love you, Mama:* the words had been a little serpent that sneaked into her mama's ear, had bitten a poison bite in her mama's brains, and her mama was (yes! yes!) done with diseases now.

No one but the child had done this thing.

So now you know the reasons from the beginning to the end. Now you know why the beautiful girl wore such a hard expression: she was gritting her teeth against the

serpent that slid in her throat. She was saving the world, and especially those she might love, from the snake. No laughing, no crying, no talking at all, because love in her was a danger to innocent people. The saddest, solemnest, soberest child in all the world: on account of love, she determined never to open her mouth again.

Part Three

Yes, and all that is very well and good, and she might have succeeded in severity—except for that skinny, signifying salesman who paraded past her window, daily, every day. This was a complication truly in all her fierce determination. For you could frown like the Doom of God, but it didn't matter. That fool kept coming anyway.

He varied the wares in his cart. He seemed to have infinite supplies. He bellowed his business all *down* the street, but eventually he wheeled his perfect self to the dark child, mute in her window.

And look what the scam-man came selling today: flowers. Potted plants.

And listen to his jive talk: "This-shere," he declared, rummaging in his cart, "is magic for my stone sad girl!" He lifted a plant of purple-pink petals to the window-ledge. He folded his hands and winked. "This-shere's the plant to pop you free," he announced. "Oh, yeah . . . *saxifrage!*" The name itself sent him into a minor ecstasy. He grinned and clapped his hands and giggled with pleasure at himself. "Saxifrage! Whew!" He mopped his brow.

That small fit over, the scam-man applied his attentions to the girl in her window. "Sacks of what?" my baby asks with the blinkin' of her eyes, on account of she got a stone mouth an' can't do nothing but blink her eyes—

The poor girl tried hard to cease all blinking of the eyes.

"Sacks, my baby wonders, of *what?* Well, I tells her, don't I? Sax-i-*fridge,* says I, all full of my smartness. Pretty girl, this-shere's a plant of magical powers. It crack the stones, they say, by touch alone. Able, they say, to cut what iron cannot bite—and they say truly. An' maybe," the scam-man whispered in a low voice, "when I slip on down the street, you catch a notion to sniff the flowers. Maybe you put your lips to the petals. An' then what? Whoop!" he shouted. "Then my magical plant crack open yo' stony mouth. 'Cause that's what it does. It breaks rock. Whoop!"

He flew into a spiral dance over the wonderfulness of his plant.

In that same instant the child sneaked a peek at the delicate, pastel flowers—but the scam-man saw her interest and was immediately at her window. In a serious voice he murmured, "I know your affliction, girl. And you should know, it don' scare me none, no, not a bit—"

But straightaway, even before she could lift her eyes, the skinny fool was back to dancing. His serious word had come and gone so swiftly that she wasn't sure if he had spoken at all.

"And how," he roared, "do a plain street hawker come up with such a thing as saxifrage? Well, lemme tell you, girl." *Clap!* The scam-man made his dance an illustration of his story. He acted out all the characters; and when he told of woodpeckers flying, why, he seemed himself to fly.

"Here's what he do, and here's what he done: he track my brother woodpecker to the woodpecker hole in a tree!" *Clap!* "When the woodpecker flit away for food, the man, he climb and plug that hole." *Clap!* "My brother woodpecker, he come home to find his hole as hard's a rock, so he fly away again, looking for . . . saxifrage!" *Clap, clap!*

"What the woodpecker know by nature, the poor man can find by brains. Here come the woodpecker back, the pretty plant in his beak, don't you know. With saxifrage he crack that plug. With the magical plant, he break it! An' when he don' need it no more, with that same sweet plant the smart man run away . . . to give it to his baby, oh, me, oh, my!" *Clap, clap—CLAP!*

The scam-man rolled his shoulders at his ears, rolled his head left and right, and moaned in the deliciousness of himself. "Oh, baby, that man is *me*," he fairly wept his pleasure. "An', baby, you—" he sang, now moving down the street with his cart and all his clangorous noise, "—you cain't do no better'n make a friend o' me. I am so smart. I am so wonderful. A flat-down, jump-up strap of a beautiful boy, ohhh—"

And then he was gone.

There was only the plant on the window ledge, below her chin.

And the poor girl couldn't help herself. In the silence of the street, she started to cry. The tears rolled down her cheeks to drop on the purple-pink flower, the sacks-of-something. But though she could not control the tears, she absolutely refused to open her mouth. She kept the ugliness, the writhing serpent, inside herself, imprisoned behind her teeth. Therefore, it was a miserable whimpering that she did, and not a true cry. Oh, how she wanted to love the laughing, signifying fool of a salesman. But loving him would horrify him. In her was the wicked power to kill him cold. So she kept her mouth closed and wept with a strange sound, like mewing.

Perhaps tears are the finest moisture the saxifrage could drink; for the delicate flower flourished; for every time the scam-man came by her now, the sad girl wept.

Here he came with a jewelry box filigreed in silver, but nothing was in it that she could see. He held its blood-red velvet open to her gaze and whispered, "Treasures, girl, brighter than diamonds, better than pearls. Cain't see what's meant to be heard, though. It's names, my stone sad girl: one for you, one for me."

He closed the box and left, and she watered the plant on her window ledge with tears.

Then here he came with hollow lipstick tubes, laughing and slapping his skinny knee. He swore that this lipstick could paint smiles on sorrowful lips—but only after saxifrage had broken the stone of his baby's mouth. And he said it had three colors, one for happiness, one for joy, and one as red as jubilation.

And when he left, she poured a rich, warm water on the thirsty plant.

But then the scam-man performed a trick which was no silly fiction, which nearly killed the little girl, because love, terrible love, now doubled and twisted and writhed in her chest, in her throat, at the back of her teeth.

For next he stood by her window with nothing at all to sell but his good right hand, which he raised on high between them.

"Sad baby girl," he said, "it's free for the askin'. Let saxifrage just crack the thinnest line of a smile in your hard face, and this-shere splendid, sleek, magnificent prize of a perfect hand is yours. Oh, baby girl, it want to be yours. I axed it. It said, *Yeeeah.*"

No smiling. Not the ghost of a smile. No words. No parting of her lips. But the tears began to stream down her stony face like the rivers out of paradise, and love rose up like a cobra in her throat. She wanted to gasp.

But the scam-man took the pointer finger of his good right hand and reached and touched her cheek and drew away one teardrop on the tip of his finger. And she gazed at this. He brought the teardrop down to himself and he kissed it. Then she saw that the moisture of her sorrow ran even to the corners of his lips. Love swelled straight into her mouth! Pressed at the backs of her teeth! It was terrifying! She was losing the fight. Love was just about to smash through her determination and fly out—that lunging, killing serpent!

So, with enormous grief, she pulled her head into her room, and she slammed her window shut against the scam-man and his plant, and she ran to an inside corner of the room and crouched there and covered her mouth with both hands, never to speak, never to cry, not even to sob: to be silent forever and ever.

For she loved the scam-man now. And she did not want to kill him.

Ah, pretty baby, more beautiful than all the children on earth, and sadder than any . . . ah!

Part Four

o she sat in the corner, frightened and dazed.

Sometimes her daddy came in but he sounded so woeful that she couldn't look at him.

"What can I do to help my girl?" he said.

She didn't answer, and he trudged from the room with lowly shoulders.

Scam-man, she thought, *do you see my window shut? Do you come? Do you look in this direction?*

And her daddy returned. "Once I had a wife," he groaned. "Once I had a son. Now I only have my daughter, and I'm losing her, too."

But no matter what he said, she didn't answer. She sat in the corner with her knees drawn up, her arms around her knees. And he left.

Scam-man, what is your name? If ever I called you by name, what would I call you?

And then one evening she heard a sound at her windowpane, a sharp, light pecking. *Tap tap tap.* And again, *tap tap tap.* She raised her head and listened. *Tap tap tap.*

Her daddy came and squinted at the window.

"What's that?" he said. "Well, I never did see such a thing before," he said. "A woodpecker, come knockin' at yo' winda, girl. Hum." But her father had little interest in anything these days, and he left.

A woodpecker!

Slowly the sad girl rose. Brother woodpecker, *tap tap tap*—he wasn't dangerous. She crept toward the window. The evening light was grey. The room was shadows, and the window was a rectangle of the dying light. *Tap tap tap:* she bent to peer at brother woodpecker—but suddenly stood stiff and straight, shaking with two almighty violent emotions.

It wasn't a woodpecker! It was the skinny scam-man, tapping with the tip of his finger, come smiling as proud as you please. And one of her feelings was a flood of love. Love shot from her breast to the top of her head, and she almost cried out, *You've come!*

But the other feeling was terror—that she *would* cry out anything at all.

No!

With his right hand the scam-man was pecking at the glass. In his left he was holding the purple-pink blossoms of the saxifrage. And with his eyes alone he was saying, *It's time. It's time, m'baby girl. An' what I got for you's the bes' thing that there is. Peace . . .*

Then he touched the window with the blossoms, and the windowpane melted and the wooden casement vanished like smoke.

The poor girl shook and shook, for nothing divided them now. But she couldn't move, couldn't scream.

No! No!

The scam-man, smiling still, continued to reach the saxifrage forward, into her room, toward her . . . until it brushed the poor girl's throat, and she broke indeed. She plain exploded.

"Go away! Go away!" she shrieked. "Get away from me—"

Then everything happened exactly as she knew it would.

Her words were *not* words. They were the serpent. The serpent sprang from her mouth and plunged through the air. The scam-man threw up his right hand, and the serpent bit the palm. The serpent flung its body like a single muscle round the scam-man's neck and squeezed. *Ahhh!* cried the child. There was suddenly a void in her where the serpent had been lodging. *Ahhh!* she wailed, for the serpent was strong and wrathful and wicked, and that was herself, was the length of the evil in herself. *Ahhhhhh!* she howled, no words at all, for she had no tongue any more.

The scam-man sank to his knees, strangled and looped at the throat by the serpent. No one could tear that hideous strength away. But the scam-man wasn't even trying. Instead, he was bending the serpent's head toward his mouth. With his right hand, still pierced by the fangs, he was setting the skull between his teeth. He was biting it, crushing it till the skull-bones cracked. So the snake began to shudder. It twisted belly-out and slid from the scam-man's shoulders and fell.

But the poison was in the scam-man now, and everything happened exactly as the poor girl knew it would.

The scam-man looked at her once more in the dim light, then sighed, then sat down on the walk beneath her window, his back to the brick wall, and he bowed his head and quietly turned stone. He died.

Ahhhhhhh! the poor girl wailed all inarticulate to the night. Her mother; her brother; and now her friend. Oh, hateful child! The tears streamed down the two sides of her face and splashed on the leaves of the plant still sitting there. He had plucked the blossoms, but the green leaves he had left untouched.

Ahhhhh! she wailed, and her bitter tears began to burn the leaves, and the leaves drooped.

⸙

On the following morning nothing arose. The sun did not arise. Instead, a dirty grey light lay on the city, and the streets stayed mostly empty. Maybe it was Saturday. Maybe no one had work to do.

There was a girlchild sitting in her window, framed by the brick to look like the picture of desolation. She was beautiful, her cheeks rounded brown like muffins and her face like the bread that is baked in an oven—but she was painfully beautiful, because her eyes were drowning in sadness. Her eyes were tired. She had not slept the whole night through. Her mouth was open like a coal black gap in the center of her face; open as if it were startled—but there were no words in there. Sometimes she said, *Ahhhhh*, and the tears rolled down her cheeks. But *Ahhhh* is all she said, and like the sun this little girl did not arise that day.

Neither did the small herb plant on the window ledge below her chin. Instead of rising, the little leaves hung down in a mortal droop. They yellowed. They loosened their finger-hold on their stems, and every time the child sighed, they shivered. And every time a leaf caught a tear, it sank still farther down, as if the load were more than it could bear.

Under the girlchild, under the potted plant, under the window altogether and still and silent on the ground lay a certain density, a stony something which, like all things else that day, did not arise.

Once in the afternoon a man came into the room behind the girl.

He said, "Is my ears lyin' to me?"

He said, "Did I make it up? Or is somebody sayin' somethin' in here?"

The sad girl drew a deep breath and said, *Ahhh.*

"Well, glory!" cried the man. "You prized yo' mouth open! Oh, daughter, I could cry. Talk to me. Say somethin' dear to me!"

But the only noise the child made was lamentation, and the big man bent down in pity.

"Whatsa matter, honey? Please. I'll he'p you the next step on yo' way. What can I do for you?"

She was staring out her window; so he ran there and looked out, too, and nearly giggled with gladness.

"That? Is that it? Oh, baby, that ain' nothin'. I could spend a *week* cleanin' the whole street for you, but that little heap o' junk, that little pile o' rock I can truck away by tomorra—"

"Ung!" the girl grunted, harsh and loud.

"I know! I know," the man said. "It's hard times, honey, but it's awmost over now, an I ain' gon' let you suffer no more—"

"Ung!"

"We got each other," he said. "Lemme go see if I c'n raise a truck. By tomorra. I promise." He left.

Ahhhhhhhh! wailed the poor child, and all the yellow leaves on the small plant trembled.

But then, for the rest of the day, it seemed that the girlchild was keeping a most desperate watch. Her face grew stiff with willfulness and determination. She folded her arms across her chest. She was a sentinel. She never moved from the window.

So the grey light drained away. So the evening darkness sank on the city again. So a breeze began to blow. And then two natural events took place, both of them unremarkable in the order of the universe:

The little leaves of the plant, the dead leaves, fell. The breeze had snapped them free, and now it hurried them down to the stone below. Like a soft crown they landed on the head of the stone; lightly, they settled on the places of hands and feet. Saxifrage nestled there.

And the other event was this: a child lay down her head and fell asleep. She had become too tired to watch forever.

Part Five

The sun came up in the morning. First there was the bright light, and then there came a jangling, raucous sound from the distance.

The little girl opened her eyes. Immediately she leaned out and looked down for the stone of the scam-man, but it was gone. The sidewalk below her window was empty. She jumped up. She was going to find her father and beat on his chest for anger, because he had already taken the stone away. She was going to seek and find where he had taken it.

But she only got as far as the doorway, and then she heard that jangling sound, and she stopped.

She heard words: "Y'all think it's fish I'm sellin' today, but it ain't, hee-hee!"

She heard: "You cock yo' eye to m'wares, an' you say, ''Tain't fish.' An' you say, 'What is it? Eels? Liver?' An' I say, 'No! Whoop! It's somethin' all o' y'all need 'cause few o' you got it.'"

She heard: "Words! I'm sellin' *words* today!"

And right after that, she heard: "Where's m'baby at her winda? Where's that pretty face? Where's that chil' that never yet done tol' me her name?"

So the little girl flew back to her window. *Scam-man?* Her poor heart swelled inside her chest. *Scam-man, is that you?* She stuck her head out into the street.

"Whoop! Whooop! There she be!"

And there was he—the prancing, dancing, spinning, coverting scam-man, nudging his grocery cart on up the street, bowing to shuffle a few steps, then snapping his body upright and clapping for himself, his own best audience.

The little girl popped at the sight. Her brown cheeks cracked. She grasped the top of her head with both hands and laughed through a mouth wide open, a liquid, word-less laughter, like craziness.

Scam-man!

"Whoop!"

Oh, he was a beautiful piece of a dancer! Scam-man, black as the kick of a horse, skinny as a fishing pole, flicking left and right. Scam-man, limber and loose and light on his feet, not a notion of stone about him. The jabbering, jive-talking, signifying scam-man . . . alive!

"Whoop! Whoop!"

Oh, and the man was ugly. And how the little girl did love him!

Straight to her window he danced. He thumped the ledge with his hand, like the perfect business deal had just been sealed. She laughed, delirious. He spun away and showed her his back, pumping his elbows for the sheer joy of being himself. "Oh, me, oh, my!" he moaned. "I be style! I be beauty! I be my own self truly, oh!"

She laughed and laughed.

"Saxifrage," he roared, "do crack the hardest, deep-down damndest, coldest, deadest core of any rock! 'Cause listen, listen," he said, slipping close to the window and laying his hand on the little girl's cheek, "how my baby do laugh. Jus' listen to my baby now."

It was his good right hand.

In the nearness of the scam-man, the child fell silent. She took his hand and gazed at it. There was a wound there, but it had healed. She kissed the palm of his hand, and low and slow the black man moaned, "Whooooooop. Well, baby, whoop for sure."

Then he drew his hand away. "Pretty girl, I got some wonderful stuffs in here."

He reached into the grocery cart and brought up a hollow lipstick tube. He screwed it open. Nothing there. But like an artist he applied it to her lips and hummed and whispered, "There. There, now. Her mouth is smilin', red as jubilation."

And it was. She felt the fire of smiling ear to ear on her gladsome face.

He reached again, mumbling, " 'Tain't fish, nor liver neither." He straightened and brought up a strap of something like rich toffee. But it was moist, and it shimmered in the morning light. It was supple, like silk.

"Baby, eat this."

And she did. Cool and good, like a thickening cream it was. She swallowed it, and immediately she felt full, full in her throat, full in her mouth.

The scam-man narrowed his eye and whispered, "Baby, talk to me."

Soft and sweet and as easy as breezes, with perfect clarity, the little girl said: "Yes."

Her eyes flew wide. The child was shocked at what she had done. "Yes!" she gasped. "Yes, yes," she shouted. "Scam-man, I said *Yes!*"

"An' that ain't all," he grinned right back at her. "What you got, baby girl, is a tongue in righteous condition. Ain' no kinks in that tongue, no—but words, yes, words an' truth an' chatter, yes! Speeches an' song an' a soft black rap, an' prayers an' beseechings an' praises, Amen, Alleluia! Yes! Ain' no end to the run o' language in that tongue, no. Oh, baby, baby!" The scam-man had begun to pant, was grinning, overcome by the prodigy of himself. "Oh, baby, what I done give you—well, I cain't call it nothin' but a miracle, the firs' one ever and the las' one, too. What I done give to you, pretty baby, is to talk like me. Whoop! *Whoop!*"

So then he had to go off and dance a while in the middle of the street, and she was trying to think of a song to sing as a rhythm for his dancing, since she could sing now, and then she thought to ask him, but she didn't know his—

"Scam-man!" she called. "Scam-man, what's your—"

But the scam-man threw up his hand and shouted, "One more thing! One more thing before your thing—an' sweeter than honey-wine this thing is, too."

So he reached into his cart, and he brought up the jewelry box, all filigreed with silver. And grinning like Christmas he opened it below her gaze and showed her the blood-red velvet, upon which there was nothing. Oh, but it must have been the most precious nothing in the world, judging by the way he picked it up between his fingers, the rarest nothing that ever was.

He raised it to her face and laid it lightly between her lips.

"Baby," he said, smiling like sunlight, "say it."

"Say what?" she said.

"What I give you," he said. "Baby, say your name."

The girlchild reached right through the window and grabbed the scam-man's hands.

"My name?" she whispered.

He nodded. "I need for you to say your name."

Then, gazing into his shining eyes, she said, "Mary."

"Whoop," he sang softly. "Mary."

She threw her arms around his skinny neck. She came fully out the window, and he caught her in arms as long as ropes. He embraced her, and she wept against the side of his face, "My name is Mary."

"An' now I can say," said the scam-man into this beautiful girlchild's ear, "what I been wantin' to say from the beginning of time. I love you, Mary. Mary, Mary, Mary, I love you for sure. Whooooooop."

An Adult's Tale
in Children's Clothing

I t has ever been my purpose to fashion stories which, though they are explicitly for children, can nevertheless engage the watchful adult as fully and as well. To that end I enrich the detail and the language enough to reward an adult's more sophisticated attentions (while the child, encountering words and constructions new to her, might stretch to learn them by their context, and so still follow the story without missing a step). I allow allusions to literatures which the child would never know (and does not need to know in order to enjoy the story at her level of experience and response). I develop chords of themes, as it were, the lower, more subliminal notes creating a fundament of which the child is no more aware than she is of the foundations of her house, but which adults might interpret with full awareness.

"Branta and the Golden Stone," for example, is explicitly a Christmas story which can be experienced by a child at the level of an animal tale, fabulous, with an element of shape-shifting at its core, whether magical or else divine. At the same time, the story (by the image and event of a lyric poem, rather than by discursive reasoning of a treatise) contemplates both the incarnation itself and the Eucharist, which are intimately connected: for we may be grateful for the flesh of the first, but we participate in the flesh of the second. "Elisabeth and the Water-Troll," likewise, is something like the tales collected by the Grimm brothers (not quite "fairy tales," as the English call them, but better designated, as the Germans do, *Kinder und Hausmärchen:* "Children- and Household-Tales"). It is modeled upon the conventions of those tales. Children can experience the prejudices and the hypocrisies of blind (adult) societies; can recognize love behind the "ugliness" which societies impute to the figures they cast out (the fat, the "dirty," the other race, the other religion); can move with Elisabeth from sadness to hope after all (or else with the Troll from being misunderstood to accomplishing heroic deeds) all of which are already the stuff of their independent imaginations.

At the same time, this story investigates the effects of an unexamined self-righteousness even as (in association with that, *and* in opposition to it) the story contemplates several varieties of death *and* the venerable sacrament, the dramatic practice of Baptism—for a dying and a baptism are also intimately connected.

In these two tales the greater weight is given to children. It really doesn't matter whether anyone notices the subtler themes that they develop (and which serve indirectly to structure them). As with "Solomon Grundy," I like the romp, and the romp is enough.

"Saxifrage," on the other hand, shifts the balance of its weight from children to adults. It represents something of a divergence: rather than being a children's story in itself, it is *modeled* on the form and the conventions of children's stories, while its intent is something more sophisticated.

Children can and do enjoy it. "Saxifrage" is a talk-story, meant to be heard out loud, because the sound as much as anything else—the rhythms, the swift successions of consonants and vowels, the street dialect, the crunchings of its contractions: the *music*—declares character, effects mood, and carries the story forward. Sense is communicated by how it sounds as well as by what it says.

But within that form the true object of this story is children. The mind of the child. More than *for* her, it is *about* her (and therefore the form, it seems to me, is most appropriate, artistically and thematically).

I've written earlier in this volume of the variety of sources for story ideas: the metaphors which children already use ("Daddy, your work eats you up"), my own remembered experience, the needs of the children whom I love, the countless relationships in which the writer lives his life. Well, here's another.

"Saxifrage, the Break-Rock" is a story-rendering of certain insights gained from the French psychologist Jean Piaget. After countless interviews with children ages three to thirteen, he mapped the natural, developmental progress by which they interpret and relate to "reality." In the book which recounts those interviews and contains his own interpretations, *A Child's Conception of the World,* I found my own well-remembered perceptions identified and explained.

It's a good guess that most adults can, by reference to specific remembered events in their early childhood, find personal enlightenment (indeed, a sort of familiarity) in Piaget's conclusions.

The chapter entitled "Realism and the Idea of Participation" investigates the child's assumption that she can personally influence the "real" world by expressing her desires in gestures or self-conscious thoughts or openly spoken words.

Therein Piaget quotes the recollection of an adult woman:

One of my most distant memories relates to my mother. She was very ill and had been in bed several weeks and a servant had told me she would die in a few days. I must have been about four or five years old. My most treasured possession was a little brown wooden horse, covered with real hair. . . .

    A curious thought came into my head: I must give up my horse in order to make my mother better. It was more than I could do at once and cost me the greatest pain. I started by throwing the saddle and bridle into the fire, thinking "when it's very ugly, I shall be able to keep it." I can't remember exactly what happened. But I know that in the greatest distress it ended by smashing my horse to bits, and that on seeing my mother up, a few days later, I was convinced that it was my sacrifice that had mysteriously cured her and this conviction lasted for a long while.

Piaget recognized that for children there is a "confusion between thought and things," that they "conceive the sign as itself effective and a part of the thing for which it stands."

Words as signs, then, can by the bare utterance *cause* what they pronounce:

. . . There is absence of differentiation or confusion between the self and the external world, . . . between the subject's own point of view and external movements: thus the child imagines that when he moves, the sun and the clouds move too. . . .

    Signs begin by being part of things. . . . Later, they end by becoming detached from things and disengaged from them by the exercise of intelligence which uses them as adaptable and infinitely plastic tools. But between the point of origin and that of arrival there is a period during which the signs adhere to the things although already partially detached from them.

Piaget called this "between time" the "magical stage," when "symbols are still conceived as participating in things." He noted that, for the child in these stages:

Reality is impregnated with self, and thought is conceived as belonging to the category of physical matter. From the point of view of causality, all the universe is felt to be in communion with—and obedient to—the self. . . .

The desires and the commands of the self are felt to be absolute, because the subject's own point of view is regarded as the only one possible.

"Rain, rain," the child sing-songs with convictions of authority and royal command:

Rain, rain, go away,
Come again another day.

Or I recall how, when I was most afraid of what might come through my bedroom door, I believed that I could by my eyebeams alone hold it shut. I stared hard at its middle, at the height of an adult head, and believed that as long as I did not blink, the power of my will, driven like nails through my eyes, would render the door as bolted as if by steel rods.

Marianne Miller, a friend of my preschool days, the daughter of the pastor of the church we attended, was developmentally disabled. I didn't, of course, understand this. I thought she spoke out of mystery, from somewhere on the other, better side of sense. One afternoon while we were taking naps together in her bedroom she told me she could do a difficult and special trick, that is, both hum and cluck at the exact same time. She showed me, accomplishing the thing with her eyes closed. Nor did I argue the specialness of the trick—the genuine charm of it. For she said that by it she could stop the world. Freeze everything. Neither one of us had to explain the value of such a power in an otherwise domineering and dangerous world. I merely nodded and believed and filed the trick away for my own future protection.

But for children these powers are themselves potentially dangerous.

For what if you give voice to an evil thought? What then?

And what if that manifest expression actually changes the "real" world?

What if, for example, you wish the death of someone, even though the wish is swift and accidental and immediately withdrawn—and then that someone dies? Whose fault is that?

Ah, the poor little girl in "Saxifrage": it is *her* fault. And she is not an isolated case. Often enough do children suspect themselves for having caused some terrible consequence.

And how can someone ease her? Release her? "Save her," as it were, from her "sin"?

Why, by taking it unto himself, the cause and the consequence both together. And now our story's metaphor expands to imitate the ancient story of an entire *Volk*, a people by which narrative they have experienced, in the telling of it, ease and release and salvation: the Christ-story, which is called the Gospel.

Riding the Horse Whose Name Is I Am

Sometimes in sorrow, sometimes in joy, if a person can stand erect and perfectly still upon the yellow plains, he will hear the whole earth drumming. He will feel the beatings in his feet and hear the song along his bones. It is as if the earth were stretched like the skin of a drum upon a great round frame, and the grandfathers were sitting around the edges, west and north and east and south, beating the skin with sticks as big as trees, each stick tipped with skins the size of buffalos: *BOOM BOOM BOOM BOOM BOOM BOOM BOOM!*

That music will call to an Indian heart, making it beat in rhythm. That music can cause in an Indian heart such love, such love . . . that it flies from the Indian, seeking the thing that sings, a thing to rest in.

For love, once it bursts the heart, is painful; and once it begins its flight, love is restless till it finds its proper resting place.

Part One

Long, long ago there was an Indian woman who fell in love with a black stallion. She grew so sick with love for this horse, that she said she would die if she could not own him and ride him.

It happened this way.

Early one morning the woman was standing at the drop-edge of a long, low cliff. The sun was just rising behind her, so the cliff made a shadow in the valley before her and below her—and on top of that shadow, like a single feather flat upon the earth, was her own shadow, slender and straight.

She had been standing this way since the dark and the stars, when she could see the great white *Wanagi tacanku* in the sky, the "ghost road" over which traveled the spirits of those who had died. Her husband took that road two years ago. It had been two years since her husband, the father of her son, had died.

And when the dawning dimmed the stars and brought her eyes to earth again, the Indian woman would have gone her way, returning to the village where her son awaited her—except that then the earth drum began to beat.

Just as the sun breached the horizon behind her, sending her feather-shadow westward as far as the eye could see, she felt in the earth a distant rhythm, *Boom boom boom. . . .* And she did not move.

She lifted her eyes, and there, on the western horizon, she saw a red cloud rising. A dust cloud, perhaps, burning in the early sunlight—but it was moving. It was stretching. Its southern point was going very fast, while a boiling red plume went up behind it.

What can run with such wonderful speed? she thought.

She held her breath, the better to see—and then, in a sacred manner, she *could* see. With perfect sight the woman saw at the leading point of the cloud, a horse. A pure black horse, and she thought it was the horse that made the drumming music in the earth. Oh, hooves of a flashing flint! She had never seen a creature dividing the ground so swiftly before. It took her breath away. She laid fingers at the base of her throat.

Boom boom boom boom boom.

Now the horse turned eastward, in the direction of the woman herself. He had a mane of black flames and a tail that streaked dark smoke in the wind of his own making. Sometimes he pulled short and leaped into the air, shaking his great head, then striking the earth with his mighty hooves for the pleasure of the impact; but then he thrust his head forward and broke into that low thundering gallop: a stallion. A shining, pure-black stallion!

And the woman gasped. She nearly swooned. *For,* she said, *he's looking at me!*

Before her husband had died, while yet she enjoyed his scent and his presence, laughing whenever her strong *wichasha* came riding back from the hunt, the other women of the village would nudge one another and say, "Look at Winona. Do you see? She loves him so much that her eyes go green with the loving."

It was true. When the woman loved truly, and when she laughed fiercely, her dark eyes flashed a deep green fire. And this was a thing her son had early learned to watch for, because green in his mother's eye meant good days for him.

But neither her son nor anyone else in the village had seen the green in Winona's eyes for the last two years. That light had gone out—

—until this very moment.

For the booming of the stallion's hooves caused an equal drumming in the woman's heart; and the closer he came, the more she grinned; and soon her eyebrows were high, and her nostrils open, and her stomach twitching with a terrible excitement—and her eyes, they were flashing that deep green again.

For the stallion had drawn up right in front of her!

"Horse," she whispered, "you are so beautiful."

And it may be that the stallion said, *Yes,* with a nickering in his mobile nose and a heaving of his magnificent head.

The woman began to pant at the nearness of the thing, for she smelled a ginger sweat and she felt warmth on the skin of her face.

Yes, the stallion might have said, for suddenly he rose rampant. With his forehooves he dashed the air above her, ever looking straight into her eyes, their visions dead level one with the other.

But his *Yes* became a blood-red pain, for down he came—with his black hooves down—and hard they struck the woman's shadow, right in the region of her breast, and she felt the blow, and she shouted.

And a second time he rose and ripped the air, then stamped the ground and the shadow of the woman in the place of her heart, and she cried out, and her crying was for pain and for love together.

And when the stallion rose and fell like the heaves of a black storm, now for the third time, Winona shaped her cry into a question:

"What is your name?" she cried.

And she asked that question because she loved him.

But the stallion had already turned from the cliff toward the western horizon and was galloping with such speed and freedom that he seemed not to touch the earth at all. He looked like a rushing black fire. But he whinnied as he went, and it seemed to the woman that he said, *I will be what I will be.* Like lightning he flew. Like thunder he drummed: *BOOM BOOM! I AM my own! I AM—that is my name!*—which seemed to the woman such an independence that it frightened her. But it split her heart with an arrow-love, with a fretful, restless love, for the stallion was already gone.

Part Two

ook at Winona!" said the women of the village that very same day. They tugged each other from their tanning racks, the scrapers still in their hands, and they pointed: "Look at her eyes! I think she has found someone to love again."

Back and forth Winona was running, grinning and giggling and pulling her son behind her.

"Do you know," she asked the young women, the women her own age, "do you know the stallion whose name is I AM? Whose coat is as black as night, but whose speed is like lightning?"

No. The young women had never heard of such a horse.

So she went to the grandmothers.

"Do you know?" she asked.

No. Neither had they heard of such a horse.

But Winona was not disappointed. Her love was also the convictions of an abiding faith.

She knelt down in front of her boy. "Would you like to fly as fast as the wind?" she said. She laughed and he laughed, and this was a gladness for all who saw it. The woman reached and stroked the small bow which her husband had made for his son three years ago. He carried it everywhere he went. "Would you like to fly like one of your arrows," she said, "from the east to the west, from sky to sky, and never touch the ground?"

The young boy grinned and touched his mother's face with the tips of his fingers.

"Oh, *hokshila,*" she cried. She drew him into her embrace. "There is a horse who, if you ride him, can make you swifter and stronger than the *Wakinyan,* the thunderbeings who live in the mountains."

Then up she was again, running to all her relatives, asking if anyone knew of the stallion and how someone might come to own him.

No. None of them had heard of such a horse.

Finally the woman went to the tepee of her ancient uncle. He was a *wichasha waken,* a holy man, whose powers came from the lowly ant: "For if you listen closely," he said, "if you know how to be attentive, even the tread of an ant can cause a drumming thunder in the earth."

Did the *wichasha waken,* the woman asked, know of the stallion whose name is I AM?

Yes. Yes, he had heard of such a horse.

"Oh, Uncle!" she cried. "Where can I find him? And how can I buy him?"

Ah, but these things he did not know. On the other hand, the terrible old woman named Wakanka, he said to his great-niece with his eyes averted: Wakanka, who was cursed by Sky ever to be stronger than a man and never to die, she may know. She lives alone in a cave in the mountains.

The holy man then raised a warning finger and said, "She gives good fortune to those who deserve it, but ill to those who don't. And always, she tells the truth."

Straightaway the gladsome woman cooked a little *wojapi,* a fruit soup, which she poured into a watertight bladder. She tucked the bladder in a parfleche bag to keep it warm, and then ran from the village toward the mountains. She climbed and climbed until she came to the cave of Wakanka.

There she opened her gift of soup. She let the aroma steal into the cave, and she called, "Wakanka, I have come for wisdom and advice."

Sniffing, sniffing, there crawled from the cave a woman so old and wrinkled that her face seemed angry, like the frowning mountain itself. One eye was blind. The other one glittered with suspicion.

She said nothing. She glared.

Young Winona gestured toward the soup. "For you," she said.

"Why?" said the old woman. Her voice croaked like the voice of a raven.

"Because I am looking for the stallion whose name is I AM."

"Why?"

"Because I wish to ride him. I wish to buy him."

"Why?"

"Because," she whispered, "I love him."

"How much? How much do you love him?" That single glittering eye was like an eagle-bone needle, to pierce the young woman at her forehead.

Blushing and bowing, she whispered, "With all my heart and with all my soul and with all my mind and with all my strength."

"Hmph!" snorted the old woman, and like an eight-legged spider she scurried toward the soup and drank it down without a breath.

Then Wakanka turned her angry eye upon the young woman again. "The horse who calls *himself* I AM. Yes! As much as you love him," she said, "that is the cost of him. For you to ride that stallion, it will cost you everything that you have."

"I can do that!" cried the woman. "I can surely do that!"

Up she jumped. Down the mountain she ran. She raced into the village, laughing as she came.

There, immediately, she gathered together everything that she owned: clothing, tools, the buffalo-horn knife that had been her husband's, her bedding, her precious quill-work moccasins, the sway-backed pony which she and her son had used for transport. . . .

The boy was watching his mother. He was laughing with her, his cheeks made round with gladness, his bow shivering and dancing in the crook of his arm. But then, when next she began to rush around *selling* all her possessions for corn and sweet grass and things a strong horse loves to eat, the boy wrinkled his brow.

"Why are you doing this?" he asked.

His mother kissed him. "*Hokshila,* it will be worth it," she grinned, the eager green shooting forth from her eyes. "Such goodness is soon to come into our lives! We will have a horse stronger and more beautiful than any creature you have ever seen. With such a treasure, what need will we have of anything else?"

So she sold everything; then she climbed the craggy mountain again and laid her pile of foodstuffs before the ancient Wakanka.

"There," she said, her breathing glad and rapid. "There is everything I have, so that I might own the stallion now and ride him like the wind."

Wakanka's one eye flashed with anger. She clawed at the blind eye and croaked: "Not enough!"

"What?" said the young woman.

"How much do you love the stallion?"

"I love him with all my mind and strength—"

"Mind and strength!" screeched Wakanka, now raising her claw between them. "Mind!" she snapped, pointing at Winona's head. "Strength," she snapped, pointing at her breast. "Everything you have, *Winyan,* means everything inside you, too!"

"Ah," said the young woman. "Yes," she said, ashamed that she hadn't thought of it before: everything included her skills, her talents, her abilities, all that she could *do,* for love that can be spoken outward goes deeply inward, too.

So she walked back down to the village, considering how great was the task before her.

And the first thing she did was to find her boy and take him to her bosom. "*Hokshila,*" she whispered. "Please go hunting for me. Take your precious bow and bring me back some porcupines. As many porcupines as you can find. I will be waiting."

With his bow, then, and with a full hunter's count of arrows in his quiver, the boy went forth, hunting from morning to night—while his mother cut and sewed fresh parfleche bags and peculiar moccasins with lacings to rise four hands up a narrow leg, and leggings too, and a great blanket. She mixed dyes of bloodroot, wild plum bark, and blueberries, so that, when her son returned with porcupines, she was ready to do the thing she did best: quillwork.

All night long she washed and soaked and flattened porcupine quills by biting them between her front teeth. She dyed them twenty different colors. She wove them into the materials she had already made. She created pictures of astonishing beauty and meaning: pictures of a smoky stallion, a being whose eyes looked straight back at all who viewed the artwork, causing them to shudder and to tremble at his glory. Moreover, the horse was wild and willful and so truly free that he seemed ready to leap from the leather and thunder away through the night.

Butterflies and dragonflies worshiped the horse. Water lilies and chokecherry blossoms bowed down before him. Even *Mato* the bear and the wolf-people and the very hunters and warriors of her own village stood in wonder around him.

By morning her teeth were worn down to the gums with chewing. And her fingers had lost their use on account of their bleeding. And the woman herself was exhausted and empty. And the villagers did not praise her for her marvelous quillwork, because it seemed to them that it mocked them by their smallness before this horse whom no one had ever seen before.

Eating nothing, drinking nothing, the woman gathered her work together and made her way up the mountain again, up to the cave of Wakanka. There, in silence, she poured the horse's food into the parfleche bags; she arranged the four peculiar moccasins in the pattern a horse maintains when he stands still; she placed a legging upon each moccasin, then laid the blanket over all, precisely as it would soon lie on the back of the black stallion.

Wakanka watched the woman. She looked at all the designs, her one good eye growing wilder and angrier all the while.

Finally Winona sat down for weariness and said, "There. This, now, is everything I have, outside of me and inside of me. There is no more."

"Not enough! Not enough!" shrieked the ancient Wakanka.

"Oh, Mother, but it must be," Winona whispered. "My hands are bloody and empty. My strength is all dried up. I have nothing, nothing left."

Wakanka lowered her wrinkled face. The mouth opened up and a horrid cackling came out.

"Hee hee! Hee hee! And how much do you love the horse?"

"I told you. With all my heart—"

"Ha! With all your *heart!*" the old woman screamed. "But when you go back down to your village, *Winyan,* what of your heart will be waiting for you there?"

It was at this moment that the woman named Winona began to cry, for she understood. She cried, and she could not stop crying.

So much did this love cost her, that she entered the village still crying, for here came her son to greet her and to receive the embrace of her own greeting in return. But she did not embrace him. She hardened her face against him. She took his hand and, without once looking at him, she led him to the tepee of her uncle, the *wichasha waken.*

When she entered the tepee, they looked at one another with a terrible knowledge and sadness, the old man and the weary woman. Only the boy did not understand.

Winona said, "He must be yours now, Uncle. He can no longer be mine. You must raise him in my place."

Then she turned toward her boy. But even now she did not embrace him. Rather, she removed the bow from his shoulder and the quiver from his back; and, bending down to the doorway, she went out of the tepee alone.

"Mama!" the boy wailed behind her. "Mama!"

But she kept walking on and on. She walked up and up the difficult path, until she knelt down before the wicked old Wakanka and laid the bow and the quiver of her son between them.

She bowed her head and waited.

But Wakanka said nothing.

A long time passed.

Finally Winona raised her eyes and saw that there had gathered in the one good eye of the ancient woman a little water. Even while she watched, a tear spilled over and moistened the wrinkles in Wakanka's cheek.

Winona, in astonishment, whispered, "Not *yet* enough? Oh, Mother, what else could there possibly be?"

It was as if sorrow itself then uttered Wakanka's question upon the mountain: *How much do you love the horse?*

She answered, "With all that I am—"

Wakanka nodded, opening both her eyes. The milky one—the blind white eye— now seemed to see even into Winona's soul, saying: *All that you are.*

Winona whispered in a ghostly voice, "Me? The cost is even me?"

Wakanka, blind and seeing, gazed at her.

"I love the black and beautiful stallion," Winona whispered. "I love him with all my being. But, Mother! If someone must spend her very self for the horse, then who is left to ride him?"

The ancient Wakanka sat still. She did not move. Perhaps the only thing left living in the woman was her eyes, for they watched Winona with, it seemed, the compassion of *Maka,* the earth.

"Mother, if I no longer am, how can I be his rider?"

And then it seemed to Winona that the stones themselves breathed the words: *Ah, we will see what we will see.*

Part Three

It was the drumbeat that awakened the lad and drew him forth from his tepee. It was the drumming he felt in his bones while he lay aground, and then in his feet while he walked, for surely it came from outside the buffalo hides of the tepee. But once he was outside, it seemed to come from the very rim of the earth.

BOOM BOOM BOOM BOOM BOOM BOOM BOOM . . .

The lad walked through the night westward, following the shimmering ghost road that crossed the sky from the east to the west.

He walked until the dawn sent a grey light through the sky, and then he found himself at the edge of a low cliff. He might have dropped down and kept on walking, but he didn't. He stopped and stood perfectly still.

He had borne no weapons with him, and he was mostly unclothed in the chill air, except that his braids were wrapped tightly in strips of the beaver's pelt. He had come humbly, then; but this was because the great drumming of the whole earth seemed a sacred thing, requiring reverence.

Soon the sun's light broke behind him, shooting golden arrows past him to the western horizon, where they struck cloud and burst into a rising red flame.

"Oiyaaa!" he breathed, for the cloud was being kicked into glory by a single striding figure. Something, someone, was tearing south along the line of earth that touches the sky.

What can move with such a power? What can shake the whole earth with its tread?

The Indian lad bent forward, then laid a hand against his lips: a horse! A magnificent horse!—and it was leaning leftward now, turning toward the east, galloping directly at the lad himself. *Oiyaaa!*

The Indian's breathing quickened. Laughter began in the lower regions of his torso: for that horse, it sheared the air! It ripped the morning like lightning, so fleetly did it run!

"Ha ha!" the lad shouted. He waved his arms and whooped a huge *HALOOOO!* And the black horse likewise raised its head and shook its fiery mane and whinnied as if in laughter, too.

And this was remarkable, for the lad had not laughed in five long years. When he was younger his mother had lifted his spirits with her joy and her love and her bright, wild dreams. But five years ago she had gone away, and he had stopped laughing—

—until this very moment.

For the shock of this stallion, the thunder of the horse's coursing straight toward him, overwhelmed gloom and grief and heavy memory.

And look! Though it was riderless, there was a riding blanket laid across its back— as if an invitation!

And look! The marvelous creature was gazing into the Indian's eyes, person to person, a sacred connecting.

But next, when the stallion had pulled up not ten feet away from the Indian lad, the lad began to cry. He went down on his knees, weeping. And the horse stepped forward, bowing and nickering, until it had closed the separation and was with its soft snout nudging the lad's face.

The eyes of the horse that were touching the boy—the eyes were a deep, deep green.

"Mama," the lad said, embracing the creature's beautiful neck and laying his head beside the horse's head. "Oh, Mama, you came back for me."

Part Four

That same night it was a whole village that heard drumming in *Maka,* the great round earth. All the people of that village were drawn outside their tepees, expecting a storm, expecting to see the lightning that caused this earthly thunder.

Instead, they saw a white moon and a black sky all filled with stars. Not a cloud. Not a breath of wind. The drumming, then, began to trouble their hearts.

But then a woman cried, "Look! Look!"

Everyone looked where she was pointing up in the night sky, and there they saw, blotting the stars of the *wanagi tacanku,* the figure of a galloping horse with a rider on its back.

The moonlight lit the rider's face like silver.

"Who is that? Who had died?" the people murmured.

But the ancient holy man of that village answered, "No one has died. It is only my nephew."

The people stared at him in astonishment.

But the *wichasha waken* only smiled and lifted his eyes in pride to the thunder above. "My great grand-nephew: he and his mother have learned how to ride the wind."

An Ethic for Aesthetics

he *Book of the Dun Cow* was published in 1978 by the Junior Books Division of Harper & Row (as HarperCollins entitled itself in those days). This was my own first book of any significance. It was written in a rollicking, unself-conscious enthusiasm. Simply, I was doing on a larger scale what I had been doing all my life till then: making up stories. Telling them. Writing them down.

Time has passed. With this present volume I shall have published more than thirty books, which together represent most of the literary genres: novels, short stories, poetry, expository prose, drama, devotional literature. Children's books. Through the length of such activity, an author is not likely to remain unselfconscious about his craft and his career—and I have not.

Moreover, for the last ten years I've been teaching creative writing at Valparaiso University.

In other words, I not only do what I do, but I've also been required to step outside the doing in order to contemplate it with some objectivity, to talk about it, to define it, and to pass it on to others. "It." This identifiable human endeavor: art. And within the wide realm of art: writing.

The definitions resulting from these contemplations I call "working" definitions. Art is as living and elusive as the cultures that produce and preserve it, the communities, the sacred communions; art, then, resists absolute classifications. And the creative process itself is ultimately too personal to be reduced to something like a universal system.

"Working" definitions, I say, first because they are what works today, but tomorrow may be subject to change; and second because their value is essentially pragmatic. It is within these definitions that I work; it is by them that I can communicate something of this work to others, to fellow artists, to aspiring writers, to intelligent readers curious about the development of the material they read.

In this essay I will outline these definitions—together with the principles which I believe them to impose upon me and my writing—because they govern the production of my children's stories as much as anything else I write.

Part One: What Is Art?

As far as I am concerned, art occurs. It happens. It is always an *event* rather than an object—though it is by means of objects that art takes place.

The painting, then, that hangs in a nighttime darkness on the museum wall is not itself art. It is a medium *for* art. When the lights come on, when a viewer steps before the shapes, the textures, and the colors composed upon the canvas, when the viewer enters the thing by playing her sight from part to part of the painting—that progressing *event* is art.

Likewise, when this book is closed and unread, it has the *potential* to become art, but it still awaits the moment of its happening. It waits for a reader. It waits for you.

Art is its own peculiar form of human communication.

As such, the complete event is divided into two parts: first, the artist acts. Second, the reader experiences. First, the artist (after long preparation, in craft and in life, both consciously and unconsciously, drawing upon life-long wisdom, insight, memory, and yet upon knowledge gathered for this present project) acts by composing the medium for this particular communication, arranging the parts and particulars to which the viewer or reader will react. The artist paints. Or conceives a cathedral (within which conception a multitude of other artists carve, sculpt, engrave, build, color and cut). Or dances (making of the shape and the movement of her body a medium for the immediate reaction of her audience). Or puts words to paper and detail to narrative.

The artist is well advised to work in the knowledge that his work will not be finished till it finds its audience. Only so does he move outside himself, into community, communion, culture (or his work may exist in his eyes only, satisfying the self perhaps, but perishing, too, with that self). Only so does he acknowledge the "other" who will also shape the thing growing under his hand. And in remembering the "other" he will recognize certain basic obligations.

First, the artist composes. Second, the reader participates in this composition of sensible detail—details which are able to be sensed, imagined, felt: *experienced.*

To my definition, then. Altogether, in its full completion, I define art as "composed experience."

But this particular experience—the artfully designed experience—is peculiar among the great, undifferentiated blends of general human experience. As I've argued in essays throughout this book, it is a "shaping" experience, more powerful for forming a person's (a child's!) sense of truth and of self than plain teaching can, or than the rest of her daily life can.

For *this* experience is discrete, having clear beginnings and endings, being separated from the rest of the day, and receiving therefore an especially concentrated attention, a peculiar wholeness of the child's attention.

And *this* experience has an internal integrity. I mean that there is not a detail in its world which is accidental or extraneous. And no detail important to the story is left out. All the details, all the sensations exert an integrated, harmonious force upon the mind and spirit of the child. The force of many details working together is like the tread of many soldiers crossing a bridge together: any single soldier on the bridge could not affect the bridge; nor would many soldiers if they broke stride; but if all the soldiers stepped in time with one another and continued marching in perfect harmony, why, the force of their rhythm could build up until it destroyed the bridge. All the parts of a story in such perfect composition can have the same effect on the child, the destruction of certain notions, the construction of others.

And *this* experience involves the whole of the child: her calculating mind, all her senses (in the cauldron of her imagination), her affective heart and emotions, her moral judgments, her body in motion and laughter and fearful anticipations and cuddling and drowsiness.

If this is the "shaping" experience, then; if its effect can ultimately help compose the perceivings, if not the character and the identity, of a child, then I find myself as the artist not entirely free! A self-satisfying, completely self-determined freedom could damage her. In order to be a good artist, I am already under certain aesthetical obligations. But I wield a powerful tool. In order, then, to compose "good" experiences for the child, I believe I am under certain *ethical* obligations as well.

If anyone questions the power of art to change reality, let him consider what propagandistic cinema, music, architecture, verse, rhetoric have done to whole populations when demagogues desired to go to war (or when democracies are themselves at war). And miscomposed stories have justified unjust behavior (as the story of Noah's curse upon his son Ham once justified slavery in my own native land).

In his essay "Religion and Literature," T. S. Eliot writes:

"The fiction that we read affects our behavior toward our fellow men, affects our patterns of ourselves. When we read of human beings behaving in certain ways, with the approval of the author, who gives his benediction to this behavior by his attitude toward the result of the behavior arranged by himself, we can be influenced towards behaving the same way."

And when the audience that experiences the literature is youthful enough, he says,

"what happens is a kind of inundation, of invasion of the undeveloped personality, the empty (swept and garnished) room, by the stronger personality of the poet."

I observe certain ethical obligations, then.

But because art is itself a living thing, I don't consider myself obligated to rules which are fixed and absolute. That would be deadly indeed. Rather, I believe that as an artist I enjoy mutual relationships with the principles embraced by these obligations, aesthetical and ethical, and with the people affected by my art. As *relationships*, then, which may change and grow to honor the growth and the change in either party (or in both of them); as relationships in which each party acknowledges the other, making promises to the other and keeping them, I can best understand my writerly and my communal obligations as covenants.

Part Two: The Five Covenants

urely, I cannot be conscious of all five covenants while I work on a story or a novel; but they become the spiritual place and the subconscious context of the writing. I can work within them as a sprinter works within his noisy arena, or (in the case of a novel) as the long-distance runner moves within the context of his natural track, the other runners, his own immediate physical characteristics, the sense and regulation of speed, his premeditated strategems. By a thousand subtle connections and clues, the context affects the runner's run.

Likewise, the covenantal relationships which I maintain with five elements of the world within which I write: they shape the tale that shapes the children. And it is ever my effort, by a wary obedience to these covenants, to "get it right."

1. The covenant with perceived reality.

The description of this covenant is easy enough. It's the practice that's complex.

What people generally reckon as the "real" world—everything visible and experiential around them—I must observe with a dead-eyed accuracy in order to "get it" (the descriptions, the setting, the ways things actually happen) "right!"

Does the wind *really* "moan"? And if so, how? (It always requires some obstruction to give it voice, like telephone wires or tree branches or the soft sifting of dry snow.) When a woman lies on her back in bed and weeps, why would I get it wrong to write "the tears streamed down her cheeks?"

No description should come from a writer's false presumption of how the universe works. No writer can live entirely within himself and expect to present a world to his reader which his reader will trust. And once trust is lost in small things it will be lost for the story whole—and *that* would make for a genuinely lonely profession (which writing is otherwise not).

So then: the natural weather in which my story is plot takes place should never be made *un*-natural in order to accommodate the plot! These two honor and acknowledge each other (which is the organic motion of covenant). But I myself broke that covenant in my novel *The Crying for a Vision* by giving a two-foot depth of snow a crust hard enough to support the weight of a boy. Such a crust is possible, of course. I was the boy who walked on it in North Dakota. But not (as I wrote it thoughtlessly) on the same very cold day in which the snow first fell to the depth of two feet. *That* snow would be soft. It needs several days of sun and wind to harden the surface. I got it "wrong," and I didn't catch the error till after the book was in print.

If I had caught my error in time, I would *not* have grumbled for running up against a difficulty, a problem to solve. Rather, I would gladly have arisen to the challenge of this contradiction between my plot and its setting. In order to do right by both, I *should* be forced to take certain creative leaps which might move my book in directions so new and unpremeditated that I myself might be astonished! Short cuts with the real world undermine a writer's rightness.

So how *do* houses creak? And why? And when?

And what does the sadness of a child feel like? And where is the sadness located within her? And what does it look like in the puckering of her chin and the tug of her lip? And is it *ever* enough to write "she was sad" without presenting the tiny and terrible manifestations by which the observer discovers sadness (and its peculiar quality) within her?

With this last series of questions we move from the realm of the natural world into the "real" lives of human beings, our multitudinous interactions, our gestures, facial expressions, moods, developments, behaviors, loves and hates and fears and delights, the subtle relationship between our *interior* selves and their *exterior* manifestations. We move into the realm of social experience—and here especially (as this is nearly always the central stuff of a story, its force and its purpose) I must observe with a dead-eyed accuracy, in order to "get it right." For if I get this wrong, why then the entire tale will be wrong, whether it's a realistic history or a fantasy.

And how shall I observe accurately the human behavior around me?

Well, (1) without prejudice (which is a blindness already in the author's eye). And (2) with sympathy. And (3) by a scrupulous, completely honest examination of my own interior self.

That principle, "without prejudice," is hard. It is frightening, as it means to live and act in an acknowledged ignorance! But we tend to live ever *by means of* prejudice. We must, you know, pre-judge most of our situations; that is, we must assume many things about each situation we enter, or we might never be able to act within it. We think we know how a salesperson will act toward us (though we don't *really* know the woman) because we take unconscious cues from only a few things: her dress, her behavior, her language. Likewise, we think we know teachers and plumbers, folks who use the language essentially as we do, men in expensive suits, train conductors by their costumes, the waitress who cracks gum in the hollows of her molars.

But to see only what we *think* we see, as necessary as it is in daily life, would cause an author to write the narrow world inside his head rather than the broad and "otherly" world around him.

So I must practice the hard, the sometimes scary exercise of resisting pre-judging those I meet; of admitting that I do not know, that every human before me is a mystery, that I am a stranger in a strange land. This constantly causes in me the feeling I experienced when first I became a pastor in the inner city and forced myself to walk the streets in all my Euro-whiteness, in all my evident difference. It feels dangerous.

On the other hand, danger makes for sharp and watchful eyes! It tunes my ears and makes my very flesh alert. And by *this* sort of observation I can discover what these people are authentically—and how they see themselves.

After a while, it isn't danger that persuades me to pay attention; it's the willing confession of ignorance and the patient watching that must follow. For those who think they know what they do not know, will never be able to know; rather, they will put all people in their own Procrustean bed, forcing upon an infinite population only a handful of the "characters," which their parochial minds had been able to identify in the world.

So in order to "get it right," I watch *for* the truth—not *with* the truth, as if it were a donkey's tail to pin on the persons I will write about.

And I watch with "sympathy."

"Sym-pathy": it derives from two Greek words, *syn,* which can be translated "with," and *pathos,* which denotes feelings, emotion, suffering, experience. I must not only observe the details of other people, but must also *participate* with them in what the details signify. So I observe "from within" the other, as it were. Though I've never experienced my own dying, yet having walked to the end the mortal paths of others, I can write of death with a personal authenticity. Though George Eliot (whose real name was Mary Ann Evans) was not a man, yet she wrote with a trenchant accuracy from the point of view (from within the mind of) a man. Though one may not be African American or American Indian, yet the observer, cleansed of himself and able to experience the world from the perspective of African Americans or American Indians (at *their* welcome, incidentally) may write their worlds and their persons with a selfless truth.

Keats said of Shakespeare's ability to "get right" such women as Lady Macbeth and Cordelia and Ophelia, to "get right" such old men as Lear and soldiering men as Othello, that he had a "negative capability." The writer negates his self in order to write from within the place of other selves.

And *that* is accomplished, paradoxically, by having, first, with a perilous candor, examined one's truest self, and by being intensely aware of how that interior self is made manifest in exterior behaviors.

I know the sins of humankind by finding them first (the tendencies, at least, and the complex machinery of motive and action and justification) in myself. I know the affective turmoil of love by recalling the experience in myself. And the gut-knots of anger, and the sweet relief of certain tears, and the wonder of children, and loneliness, and prepubescent despair: I recall these things from within my own experience—and from having been intensely alert to them while they happened.

But more than that I, like most children, was also aware of the *signs* of these things in my own facial expressions, my posture, my tone of voice, my behavior. All such visible manifestations of the invisible experience became a language by which I could read the faces, the bodies, the sounds of *others,* and so interpret their moods, emotions, feelings: I could see into, and enter into, the interior drama. In this sense, artists *are* like children; either by nature or else by striving, they maintain the ignorance and the wonder and the immediate sympathy of the little girl who, when she sees the signs of sorrow in her mother's face, immediately mimicks those signs in her own and then (exactly like her mother) begins to weep, does genuinely weep, although she cannot know the cause of her mother's tears.

2. The covenant with the conventions and the community of my chosen craft.

I can be briefer about this covenant, though it has required a lifelong attention.

The conventions of my craft are the forms and patterns of literature's various genres. This covenant was established even before I knew it; I entered an apprenticeship of sorts when I, who read continually, became conscious of the words themselves, and loved what they could do, and started to question *how* they did it.

"Getting it right" in this case means making the words work as best they can. Making the poem a poem indeed—and besides that, a good one, too.

Sentences. Lines of verse, the sounds of those lines, the shape of many lines put together according to certain anticipations: sonnets, lyrics, hymns. Alliteration. Dialogue. Description. Suspense. The episodic progress of a narrative. Stories. Novels. Each literary form has its definitions. Each has a history, through which the definitions have evolved and changed. These are the templates and the tools of my craft. Of course I should know them—even if I choose, in any particular story, to diverge from them. Of course, I should continue to read what they have been in the past so that the tools I have to hand are ever more various, ever more accurate.

So then, my covenant is as much with the authors who have gone before me as with the tools we use in common. T. S. Eliot, in his essay "Tradition and Individual Talent," argues:

> "Tradition . . . cannot be inherited, and if you want it you must obtain it by great
> labour. It involves . . . the historical sense . . . ; and the historical sense involves a

perception, not only of the pastness of the past, but of its presence. . . . This historical sense, which is a sense of the timeless as well as of the temporal, and of the timeless and the temporal together, is what makes a writer traditional."

But this second covenant must also embrace authors who are my contemporaries. We never do write in a vacuum of our own making. At least I can't. (Maybe a writer gets to do one major work this way; but after that he'll be rewriting the same thing over and over.) Besides reading the material of this present age, I have established and maintained personal relationships with other writers—as friends, if possible; as colleagues busy about the same profession, certainly.

So I exchange communication regularly with authors like Wendell Berry, Madeleine L'Engle, the playwrights Robert Schenkkan and Jim Leonard and Mark St. Germain, the poet Robert Siegel, film-script writers and producers David McFadzean and Matt Williams. Moreover, we meet and talk when we can, and sometimes read one another's material. It is in the spontaneous interaction among artists (and, surely, artists of all the arts) that the spirit of any one writer is challenged, refreshed, revived, sustained. It is in such discussions that the work of a particular time-period gets its quality of kinship. And it has been this way throughout the history of literature, that artists talk with artists, argue, collaborate, criticize, disagree, imitate.

3. The covenant with my audience.
Of this covenant I think I am always aware. It is fundamental to any sort of communication; to art, however, it is the essential relationship, without which the artistic event remains unfinished. I write to be read. As talk is meant to dwell within the listener, so the end of all I write—its termination *and* its purpose—is the audience. Or, a sillier (more self-serving) way to say this is: the chance that a novel may be read (and perhaps praised) justifies the time and the serious, wearisome labor it takes me to produce the thing in the first place.

In the case of this third covenant (as implied by most of the essays in this book) my obligation is to "get it right *for the sake of*" another.

So, then, I seek a relationship that may entertain you; that could possibly enlighten you; that might elevate, might even ennoble you; that should, will ye, nill ye, expand your experience, granting you new eyes upon the "real" world around you. . . .

I seek, in other words, a relationship that could, in a manner sane and unsentimental, love you. Yes: though it is by its very nature not a visible thing, and though no one else need realize the motive which rests within me—which drives me, even as your reading draws me—writing is as much an act of love for the reader (one by one by one) as it is for the craft itself. And writing for children in particular is an act of *intimate* love: for when I write I cannot conceive of auditoriums full of children, nor of that abstract collective, "children." I think of child. This one child. This other child. Individuals who will *as* individuals in close relationship with the adult that reads to them—or, if they read on their own, in close relationship with my own voice—enter my tale and dwell there for a while.

And what this cardinal covenant of love requires of its parties in any circumstance, it also requires of me as the artist who shapes and who names for the sake of the tender reader.

I must not abuse the subtle power of art.

I must not indulge in the abuse of power called propaganda; that is, in the cynical effort to make people—whole groups, whole communities—believe what is a lie. For because art shapes those who receive it uncritically, the people would then *become* the lie. In this way, art can damage. It can enslave both the minds of the readers and those whom the readers control, who are the objects of the artistic lie.

I must tell the truth. Its alternative is devastating.

T. S. Eliot:

"It is literature which we read with the least effort that can have the easiest and most insidious influence upon us. . . . [T]his reading never affects simply a sort of special sense: it affects us as entire human beings; it affects our moral and religious existence."

Do you recall my discussion of art's ability to "name" in the essay "The Writing of Branta and Other Affections"? I said that to name a thing is to grant that thing three necessary benefits: to make it known in the human arena; to grant it blessed and effective relationships to every other named thing in the universe; and to declare its purpose, and thereby its value, in the world.

But what if the story is a lie? And what if the name that people accept and utter thereafter conceals the truth?

Why, then it can in whole groups, whole communities and cultures, conceal the truth of the child so misnamed. It can hide the truth of her person, her real character, her purpose and her *value,* even from herself. Moreover, the true child would then be isolated, cut off from the rest of society, as well as from the blue firmament and the green earth and the gathered seas! For if the story of creation in Genesis 3 is construed to mean that Eve is responsible for the fall of all humankind—and if the telling of this tale names and characterizes *all* women according to a primordial fault—what must be (what, in fact, has been) the effect of such false naming upon women themselves? Ah, what a loneliness! What an incarceration. Even the apostle Paul did not interpret the fall in this manner. But ages and ages of cultures have, destroying the truth of womanhood—and thereby of women—through cruel millenia of human history. And a story is at the source of it.

But if that example is rather too cosmic for the lowly children's tale, then consider Hugh Lofting's innocent book, *The Story of Doctor Dolittle,* which I in my childhood read with a happy hunger. I dwelt in the tale. I, only barely conscious of my identity as an American white boy, traveled with Dolittle down to Africa. The animals were not dangerous. They were just needy—and we, Dolittle and I, could satisfy them. I recognized the fantasy, and I delighted in it. But then Dolittle was locked by an African chief in an African jail. He got out, of course. By a cunning trick.

It's that trick which left a lasting (albeit unconscious) impression upon me. For though it was accomplished by an unreal exaggeration, there was at the core of the trick an insight which I received as the fundamental truth upon which Lofting's fantasy was built. (Fantasy, in order to work, must always derive from realistic propositions of human nature and the nature of this world.) The trick? Dolittle promised the son of the chief that if he would let the doctor out of jail, the doctor would turn his black skin white. He mixed a brew of everything white in his medical bag, and had the black child dip his face into it.

Of course the trick worked; for don't little black boys see little white boys as the better thing to be? The "naming" that took place here entered me at the same deep level as my sense of my own whiteness: barely conscious, but pervasive and central to my more spontaneous definitions and decisions. I continued satisfying in my racial (if not my own personal) superiority.

But this must be my covenant: by means of my writing to love *all* children, each and each—the one who reads as well as the one affected by the reading.

The apostle Paul speaks of edification—an interweaving and an upbuilding of the community—as coming from "speaking the truth in love."

4. The covenant with my community at large.

As an officer of the law is a functional citizen of his community, whether he deals with ten people or with ten thousand, so am I an active citizen of mine, even though no more than ten people may have read what I've written. But (1) because my work can't help from reflecting my context and my community, and (2) because that work goes far beyond the community itself, and (3) because my attitude regarding my artistic profession affects the way I affect friends and citizens around me—it is right that I acknowledge a covenant of honor between me, my work, and the people among whom I live and write.

Too often, and too easily, artists have seen themselves as creators not unlike the first Creating Deity. Or, if they do not rise to divinity themselves, they worship their "muse," their talent, the transcendent experience of inspiration, their profession as if *it* were divine. Everything else pales before the supreme act of artistic creation. And because all the life around them may be material for their art, they can feel justified in sacrificing any tender part of it on the altar of this exalted profession (or else they may not even notice how they cut and burn living things for the sake of this obsession). Their art, then, feeds upon their community. It can consume friendships and families and spouses ever before it—the artistic project—is complete and available to a broader public.

Communities, too, are at fault, often elevating the more famous artists among them to celebrity status: actors, movie directors, *best*-selling authors, dancers, singers, songwriters. And if such a treatment is at least a potential for the more minor artist, he may take on airs before airs are granted him—in which case the damage is perhaps solely his own.

For my sake, then, as well as the sake of the communion in which I live as a busy citizen not different from the cop on the corner, I keep covenant with my family, my people, my church, my town, my commonwealth: I honor what they in good faith honor. I honor what is honorable among them. At every level, both as an artist and as a member of the communal body, I participate.

Or, to put this another way, I do not objectify them, divorcing my own accountable self from them in order to study, scrutinize, criticize, examine, analyze them, as if they were a smear on the scientist's microscopic slide.

Here is what careless, uncovenanting art can do:

I know a woman who lives in a large house in a small town in Michigan. To the delight of everyone, a movie crew arrived to film the village, its streets and shops and houses, as the setting for a full-length feature. This woman's house received more camera attention than any other in town. My friend was flattered—until the movie itself was released to theaters nationwide. She went to see it. And she returned home ashamed. For her house had become the home of vile, ruinous people. It stigmatized the building for a little while, which caused her some local distress. But worse than that, she believed that her dear place had become in the imagination of the nation a place of wickedness and horror.

I myself became intensely aware of the need for this fourth covenant while I was doing research for a novel about the Lakota Indians, *The Crying for a Vision.* Marlene Whiterabbit Helgemo, an Indian herself and a friend of mine, invited me to spend time with her on the Rosebud Reservation in South Dakota, specifically to attend the Sun

Dance there of a holy man named Elmer Running. She had said, "If you are serious about this, I will invite you to our religious ceremony." I accepted, never doubting that this would be the best sort of research I could accomplish.

"Research," I say—until I drove between two tall poles marking Elmer Running's ranch, and down a dirt road to a wooden hut, where three very large Indian men approached and motioned for me to stop.

I rolled down my window.

They wore their black hair long and braided. I saw thick, hypertrophic scars on their breasts and their backs. They gazed at me a while.

Why was I there, they asked.

I told them that Marlene had invited me.

"Do you have a camera?"

"No."

"Do you have a tape recorder?"

"No."

I was telling the truth. It hadn't occurred to me to bring either one.

"Do you draw?"

That was a different sort of question. And though in their minds it had a similar purpose, in mine it had ceased to consider mechanical devices and had begun to consider *me,* and my purpose for coming among them.

"No," I said. "I can't draw." *But I can,* I did not say, *take notes.*

They let me pass.

And I readjusted completely my relationship to them and to the experience I was about to enter.

I had intended to scrutinize, to examine these people, to make them the objects of my researches rather than to seek in them subjects of a fully human relationship with me. But they themselves had already experienced the faintly insulting experience of anthropologists working among them. No, not "among" them, but "upon" them. With a twinkling contempt, they call such human ciphers "Anthroes." Merely to study the sacred rituals of a people, you see, is to demean them, to deny the genuinely holy quality of the ceremony. What the Lakota know as a sacred way to dance with the eternal and to join the limit*less,* the anthroes reduce to a particularized, limited, definable practice of a primitive people. The scientist might truly admire what the Lakota do; might acknowledge a complexity in the act and a pragmatic consequence; but they would never subject *themselves* to it, body, heart and spirit; and the absence of faith in them makes them, the anthroes, seem like dissociated and foreign spirits in this place.

I took no notes. I dismissed the book from my mind. I subjected myself completely to them and their community; subjected myself, I must confess, in some fear—but fear is the poor man's humility for it does, after all, make him alert to all things around him, visible and invisible.

In other words, I became intensely conscious of the covenant which I as an artist must keep with all those who may enter my writing and thereby enter communities not confined to *this* place and *this* time.

The lack of a complete, complex human relationship between the artist and the communities that enter his art—the lack of a covenant of mutual obligations—can be cruel. Those who are only scrutinized may feel as if they've suffered a theft. Something significant to their identities has been taken and handled, *hand*-dled, man-handled. Now, that significant thing may never have known its name before. The artist might have brought it to surface, allowing a community to see in itself what it had not noticed before (for this *is* the artist's skill, to name the hidden things). But unless this has been accomplished for the sake of the community, the artist has—by the very act of naming it, discovering it, as it were, and peddling it abroad as his own—the artist has, I say, assumed an ownership of the community's precious things as well. A shared ownership need not be baneful, unless one of the two owners owns coldly, without a devotion to the thing he takes in his hands to sell away. If it was something beautiful, its beauty is compromised by having been plucked from the ground that nourished it. If it was a secret grief or a concealed sin, well, the god to which it has been sacrificed is a god that doesn't redeem. This public god can only accuse.

This, then, is the core of my covenant with my community: that my writing must serve them rather than being served by them. Why should my profession be considered of any greater importance than theirs?

Ovid boasts:

Est, Deus in nobis; agitante calescimus illo:
Sedibus aethereis spiritus ille venit.

"There is a god in us," he writes of writers. "We grow hot at his urging: that spirit comes from thrones ethereal." Such an attitude has existed in Western societies for ages, that there is a divinity about the artist; that art is his worship; that such worship carries all before it.

But in other societies—African, American Indian, Inuit—the tale-teller is a *griot,* a servant of persons and of people, comforting them through long nights, acting as the memory of all, whose tales therefore are memorials.

I like this latter much better.

5. The covenant with my faith.

No artist works without axioms by which to order the whirling bits of this existence. The poet: "a heaper into heaps and a piler into piles." It is the very nature of art to arrange messes. A novel is the result of organizing, is like an organism, creating structures the reader can comprehend, *composing*, as I've said, the details and sensations which become a reader's experience.

But the artist must have certain standards according to which he makes an order (even an absurdist order) of the stuff of this life. I call these standards "axioms," because they are at the very base of his seeing; they are the *means* of his seeing; they themselves need neither proofs nor arguments to be regarded as true by the artist; rather, they become the arguments for the truth and the order of everything else.

Or to say this another way, these unquestioned standards are the tenets of his faith. Simply, he believes them. This faith may acknowledge a god. It may not. It may be orthodox or else peculiar to this artist alone.

Some artists may, by means of a spontaneous consistency within their work, for the first time come to recognize what they have believed all along.

Others are able to identify clearly and directly in expository essays the belief that also governs their art. Albert Camus is such a one, for the axioms that shape and arrange his novel *The Plague* are presented propositionally in his book *The Myth of Sisyphus.* Camus is an existentialist.

I am a Christian.

As with Camus, this is not separable from anything else I do. Surely, it does not mean that I must proselytize whenever I write, for this title defines my identity, not my intent—and proselytizing is an activity eminently separable from writing. "Christianity" indicates the axioms by which I make sense of the mess of human experience, sense enough to give it a compositional order in a story. My faith, however, doesn't suppose that I understand everything. I relate to it as in a covenant, a living, developing relationship. These are axioms by which I interpret; they are not fixed and rigid interpretations in themselves.

If either one of us, then—Albert Camus the existentialist or I myself the Christian— did not each honor our personal faiths; if we did not feel obliged to grant them a guiding role in the production of our stories and novels; if we refused to continue in covenant with these axioms and wrote what in fact we did not believe, then we would become something like mercenaries, pens for hire, putting our craft in the service of foreign "truths" for motives certainly less than artistic and possibly less than honorable. In fact, our work would be stunned at its core. We might be writers thereafter, but not artists, free and independent. And if we should so detach ourselves from this fifth covenant as to become the expression of someone else's faith or foolishness, why, then every other covenant would be broken. I have already written of the damage that can do to others, readers and communities.

Moreover, with regard to the damage to myself: if I rejected this faith, my elemental means for making decisions (in life and in writing), how could I heap anything into heaps or pile anything into piles? How could I organize, compose, or structure anything of human experience into the experience a reader could enter? How could I write at all? You see, to break this fifth covenant (even though it were not for mercenary reasons) would surely throw up in front of me the most monumental writers' block ever! It would render me wordless.

In the case of this covenant, then, to "get it right" is to get it "righteous."

For Chapman, While He Is in Hate with God

I have arranged the stories of this book in an ascending order. The first is for very young children. At the end of the volume I've placed a story prepared for youth at the other end of the age scale. This one, "For Chapman While He Is in Hate with God," is written for young adults who have begun to experience the anxieties of social identity, whether they can truly "fit in" with their peers or whether they must admit to difference, for worse or for better.

I see you sit in the dining hall, your head bowed over a dinner plate, your body tired. You buzz toward sleep.

Your roommate sits across from you. He's chewing. He has a fine appetite. You feel his eyes on you, which makes you bow your head farther. No one should be talking to you now. No one.

But he says, "What's the matter, Chap?"

"Nothin'."

"Not hungry?"

"No."

"Can I have your french fries?"

What's the matter, Chap?

But you're not thinking about the matter, are you? Because, what if you did? What if you brought the matter and all its pieces together in your brain here and now, in the dining hall? What would you do then? Maybe you would just explode.

"Chap?"

"What?" You catch a quick, scared glance at him.

"The fries? D'you want the french fries or not?"

You shrug. You shake you head. You push the plate over to him. To Alex.

"Thanks."

You shrug.

It really would be better if you slept, right? The best way to think about nothing at all is to lie down and shut your eyes and go straight to sleep. You shouldn't have come to the dining hall. But when Alex pushed back his chair and said his usual, "Welp! Wanna eat?" neither did you want to be left alone in the dormitory room. It's a crock. It's all a crock. Crock-crock-crock . . . and Brentano's.

Alex is talking while he eats. But the words blur, as if he's humming a word-*less* tune with pitches high and low. Sometimes he laughs at something he said. You don't, of course.

Suddenly you're aware that Alex has stopped talking.

Which makes you wonder why.

Which causes you to make the mistake of looking at him.

You feel a little shock: he's looking right back at you.

And before you can drop your eyes again, he says, suddenly and clearly, "You're not worried about *Lomax*, are you?"

Immediately you cry, "Why should I worry about Lomax?"—which is your second mistake in a row, to say the name, to let the name get into your mouth. But it had already gotten into your ear. Oh, you want to hit Alex. No, you want to hit yourself with a fist in the side of your head.

Quick! Think! Think about other things!

"I hate this food," you say with real energy. "I hate meatloaf. How often do we have to have meatloaf? And these boiled peas—" Peas, which you start to squash, now, like ladybugs with the flat pad of your thumb.

"It *is* Lomax," says Alex, "isn't it?"

Think! THINK! Your name is Chapman Wagenknecht. Think it syllable by syllable, Chap Man Wag—

"Ah, c'mon, Chappy, let it go! What is, *is*—is what I say."

Chappy. Your classmates call you Chappy. You'll be fifteen in February. You're a sophomore at McLean's Christian Academy. It's a boarding school for boys. You write. You write stories. This is the thing you do. This is what distinguishes you from everyone else at McLean's. Late at night, after lights-out, you crouch under blankets and write, though you've never let anyone read the stuff. And only a few boys know of your obsession. Alex does, though he considers it a harmless quirk. Haverford does, too. No teachers, though. Even your parents don't *really* know.

Alex says, "You worry too much."

And then he says, "I think you're going crazy, Chappy. Look at you."

That's when you notice that your fingers and your hands are covered with green mash, and your fingernails have meatloaf crammed beneath them. So then a series of swift thoughts flash through your brains:

That, yes, maybe you *are* going crazy.

But that (Alex doesn't know, Alex cannot know) you have an excellent reason for insanity.

That there is a roaring ocean of feeling about to break upon your poor soul, to spout and drown your soul, if ever you let the full matter of Lomax in.

And that it's taking almost all your strength and effort to keep him out.

But I know the matter, Chapman. I know it from start to now. And I know that it is not finished, though to you it seems it can *never* be finished; and that the simplest feeling to feel right now (of all the feelings you could be feeling) is anger.

You are mad. You are so mad it's eating away at your guts, so that anytime you swallow something down, you want to throw it right back up again.

Who are you mad at, Chapman? Who is it safe to be mad at?

Alex leans back and pats his tummy and grins. "Gooooood," he says. He has dark blonde curls and a blaze of pimples over his cheeks and his forehead. He gets some sort of satisfaction from popping them in front of the mirror in the john. Once he woke up and found you writing under the covers at night. He sneaked into neighboring rooms and brought four guys back to your room, and for a joke ripped the covers away, grabbed you by your underpants, dragged you into the john, threw you into the shower, and turned it on as cold as it would go. Friendly joke. They wept with laughter. And you were cold, too—but not as cold as you pretended to be, not quite *that* tormented. Why did you pretend? To persuade them of your greater suffering? And that you could take it, tougher than most? But you aren't tough, are you, Chapman?

I think you pretended just in order to keep secrets.

I think you do this a lot: conceal true parts of yourself from everyone else in the world, because you feel it is some sort of advantage never to be totally known. It's like the spy who sees but never is seen. It's like the idiot kid whom everyone assumes to be stupid, so they let him alone—but he's really as smart as a jungle cat, and can therefore get away with . . . with anything. With murder. Right, Chapman?

"Goooooooood," says Alex, who loves to eat, who is athletic and blunt and uncomplicated and content with himself, content with his whole life, if the truth be told. "Chappy!" he will cackle, poking you in the ribs till you wince and make silly giggling sounds. "Chappy, Chappy, lighten up! What is, *is*—is what I say. And you can't do nothin' about it!"

He gets up, collects his dishes and silverware on a plastic tray, and carries the mess to the dishwasher window.

So do you. You wipe your hands on paper napkins and follow.

Then you both shrug into thick parkas and go out into the snowy night where your breath makes pale angels which the wind distorts and tears away.

Someone is playing the organ in the chapel. You can hear the low tones. Haverford, maybe. He plays the organ. He practices constantly. His hair is always combed to a perfect, shining slickness. Once when you were studying in the evening in a classroom alone—no, you weren't studying, Chapman: you were trying to write a poem, remember? Once when you were striving to produce something worthwhile in a classroom, the organ in the chapel down the hall burst suddenly into fountains of sound. It took your breath away. You got up and sneaked into the back of the chapel, and there was this thin, earnest *boy,* producing monuments of music by the bare motion of his fingers; and the part in his hair was as white and as straight as the edge of a page. Haverford!

Alex glances to the right and clucks his tongue and puffs words into the winter air: "Haver-everlasting's at it again. You ever watch how he twitches his fingers, Chappy?

Ever seen how long those fingers are?" Alex elbows your ribs through the parka. "Betcha he *manicures* them. Twit, twit, twit!"

In your dorm room your roommate flicks on the radio. You bend your head over your desk and begin to translate the Latin of Marcus Tullius Cicero. Your guts have relaxed a little. You're somewhat relieved (could you admit it to yourself) to be out of the dining hall again.

Chapman? When will you allow Lomax back into your mind?

When will you finish this thing?

You will have to finish it, you know—or perhaps be stuck at this age, just two months shy of your fifteenth birthday, forever.

It was over the loud speakers affixed to the walls of the dining hall that you heard the voice of Headmaster Riemer announce the passing of Mr. Lomax. It was then—in the instant of the knowledge of his death—that all things stopped for you, wasn't it?

Cicero: . . . *autem, celeritas moriendi abstulit sensum. De quo genere mortis est difficile dictu . . .*

Chapman Wagenknecht: ". . . indeed, a quick dying . . ." This is the way you translate those first three words, but you really want to write *his* quick dying, meaning, of course, Scipio's death, the death of the great man about whom Cicero is writing here: "a quick dying . . . has taken away . . ." What? Has taken away *sensum, sensum.* Look it up: "feeling, sensation, understanding, judgment . . . thought." One of those. Now, to the next sentence. *Dictu:* "A word." *De quo genere mortis:* "about this sort of, this type of, death." *Est difficile:* "is difficult."

Mr. Lomax taught algebra to freshman boys and geometry to the sophomores. At his own request, he also acted as a faculty proctor and lifeguard during the afternoon periods of free swimming in the pool.

The top of his head was completely bald, with a fringe of hair running around the back from ear to ear. His arms, on the other hand, were perfect jungles of thick hair, reddish brown in color. Hair sprouted on the back of his fingers. Hair was luxuriant in the holes of his ears and in his nostrils. He must have shaved several times every day.

He had a soft, tenor voice, enormous brown eyes, and a sort of mopy-sad-smiling expression which Chapman definitely interpreted as an appeal for friendship from his students. To Chapman the appeal implied loneliness and hunger. It unnerved him, Chapman, because he—Chapman—recognized it as the very expression *he* would have worn if he had allowed his deeper feelings to show in his own face. He, too, felt isolated, felt not well enough—or at least not naturally enough—befriended. That expression also caused in Chapman a faint contempt for the teacher who could not act more teacherly, more independently. Chapman was embarrassed for Mr. Lomax. And it was their very likeness which made Chapman promise himself never to be seen as a friend of Lomax, as someone who might respond to that naked appeal.

When Lomax suffered his own embarrassment—which really had to go all the way to humiliation before he seemed to notice how bad a situation had become—his whole head blushed. He would be standing at the blackboard, facing away from the class, his left arm raised with a piece of chalk, in the very midst of drawing a parallel line, when the shame would dawn on him; and then he would freeze in that posture; and then his bald head would break into a beady sweat and *shine!* Shine bright red.

Already by October that year, Chapman's sophomore year, the boys at his level and in his geometry class had devised a no-fail method for causing in Mr. Lomax this terrible, burning humiliation. Chapman saw the method develop by accident, sort of. He didn't think it would have become as cruel as it did if Lomax had *not* reacted. It was the embarrassment in him that showed the boys the way to go. It was embarrassment that they scented and followed like dogs chasing some small woodland creature. And the brighter it glowed in that lightbulb head of Mr. Lomax, the more rabid did the boys become.

One day George Arbeiter said, just loud enough for a few around him to hear, "Max beats his wife."

Although his grades are poor, George himself has a native, animal shrewdness. He must have seen the tiny hesitation in Lomax's arm as it drew its line across the blackboard.

Because several days later he repeated the phrase. He put a comb in front of his lips, which gave his voice a musical, buzzing quality. So did Peter Angstrom put a comb hard against *his* lips. And softly, together, the spoke in a sing-song, liturgical fashion, "Max beats his wife. Max beats his wife." The rhythm of the phrase was somewhat infectious: TUM-da-da-DUM! TUM-da-da-DUM!

Other boys joined in.

Lomax held still a moment at the blackboard, then turned around, a truly quizzical look wrinkling his forehead, as if there were some important question he wanted to ask, but didn't quite know the words.

The moment he turned toward the class, George and Peter were quiet, attentive, respectful, studious.

Chapman, where he sat in the back, could not believe what had happened. It almost seemed a dream to him.

He knew that Lomax did have a wife. He'd seen them together when the faculty gathered in the dining hall for formal dinners with the student body; and sometimes she would sit beside him in morning chapel. A smallish woman, she was, with quick breathless movements, sitting hard against her husband's side. She seemed always frightened—but whether in life or else in public and in the presence of all these boys, Chapman couldn't guess.

By the end of October, this method of humiliating Mr. Lomax became something like a ritual. Many boys brought their combs to class. Why did it have to be combs? Chapman didn't know. Maybe it was like a costume, meant to prove that this isn't the way the boys *really* were, that they were only acting at being something else for a little while. Don't blame them. On the other hand, it surely proved that they *planned* to do the thing, each one for himself, for boys didn't usually carry combs around at McLean's.

"Max beats his wife! Max beats his wife!"—uttered in a weirdly subdued tone, half-whispered, mostly ghostly: "Max beats his wife! Max beats his wife!"

Chapman refused to join in. But he didn't reprove anyone. (Wherever would he get the authority to do that?) And he didn't sit tall in the back of the classroom so that Lomax might notice one boy "on his side," as it were. No, Chapman put his head down in the crook of his arm on the desk, and only sometimes peeped up to see the torment in Lomax's eyes.

Still, when the teacher turned from the blackboard to the class, everyone was silent, their combs up their sleeves.

But now in a whining voice—in a really contemptibly sniveling voice—Lomax would preach to the class. He would literally pull out a King James Bible and read to them, would beg them, in fact, to be loving as God had commanded them to be loving.

His voice shaky, his hairy arms trembling so much that he had to put the flat of one hand on the pages of the Bible to keep them from flipping the wrong way on him, Mr. Lomax read from Galatians. Chapman knew which book it was because Lomax had *said*, "Galatians, chapter five and verses fourteen through fifteen. God, says. Boys, please, *God* says, 'For all the law is fulfilled in one word, even in this: Thou shalt love thy neighbor as thyself. But if ye bite and devour one another, take heed that ye be not consumed one of another.'" And then he would look up. "How can you be Christians," he would plead, "if you don't love? How can this be? It will hurt *you* in the end. It will *hurt* you the most," he whined. "This will devour you. It will eat you up. It will," he said—and Chapman felt that Mr. Lomax was confessing what he genuinely believed, and that he was genuinely worried on behalf of these boys: "It will destroy your soul!"

On Tuesday the twentieth day of November, Chapman Wagenknecht, though he did not bring a comb and had not planned on it—indeed, did not even know he was going to do it—joined the classroom chorus of abuse. But he did not keep his voice subdued. He couldn't. Spontaneously, he yelled the words. He leaned into them as if they were weapons, and he hurled each one with an angry force at the heart of the teacher before him:

"Max beats his wife! MAX BEATS HIS WIFE!"

For on the day before, Monday the nineteenth at four-thirty in the afternoon, sitting on the edge of the pool, both dabbling their feet in pool water, Chapman and Lomax had shared a brief conversation.

Mr. Lomax had come and sat down beside him and, out of the blue, had said, "Midge is sick."

Chapman looked at him and frowned. *Midge?*

"My wife. Margaret," Lomax said. "She's in the hospital today and tomorrow for a series of tests. She's been sick for more than a year, now. We both suffer it."

The teacher offered these confidences with such an unselfconscious ease, that Chapman received them the same way. It never occurred to him that they might be improper, teacher to student like this. Rather, he felt flattered. Elevated. One in whom an adult could recognize unusual maturity.

He nodded slowly, looking down at his feet.

"Tests," he said.

They were alone in the great echoing room of the pool.

"It's some kind of women's condition," Mr. Lomax said, vaguely waving an arm. "We both suffer it." He looked at Chapman, which made Chapman warmly alert to how skinny and white was his own body in swimming trunks. Lomax himself seemed full-dressed in trunks, downright *furry* across his chest, over his shoulders, down his back, down into the band of the trunks themselves. Chapman noticed for the first time that his geometry teacher bit his nail to the quick.

"What about you?" Lomax said. "Are you feeling okay these days?"

Chapman turned the question over in his mind. Were any of his secrets showing? Could someone so like himself in some ways peer more deeply into him than Chapman might wish? Or *did* he wish for such companionship.

"Well," Chapman heard himself saying, "I get homesick."

"Ah, Chapman, I'm sorry." Lomax gazed at him with an enormous, brown-eyed compassion. "Do you miss your parents, then?"

Again, Chapman considered the question, then delivered a careful answer, "Well, no. No. I'm not quite sure what I'm homesick *for*."

"That's deep, Chapman," Mr. Lomax said. "That's profound."

Chapman nodded. Profound.

"I've tried to write about it," he said.

"No!" said Lomax. "You *write?*"

Chapman nodded.

"What, *poetry?*"

Chapman nodded.

Lomax, looking at him still, laid a finger beside his own chin, in which there was a cleft, in which there was red whisker stubble, hard to get at when shaving, and said with a surprising tenderness, "Why don't you come over tonight? Bring your poetry. We'll read it together."

Chapman's immediate response was a flush of gladness. He felt warmth creep into his cheeks and consolation into his heart, and his lips of their own accord began to pull back in a smile. More importantly, by turning his eyes to Mr. Lomax's eyes, he was about to offer this pleasure, together with his "Yes," directly to the man who was sitting beside him. *Yes,* he almost said. *I would love to come.*

But Lomax, too, was showing a similar flush of gladness. He, too, was grinning—and spontaneously he lifted his hand and wrapped the fingers around the back of Chapman's neck.

That touch, by its very tenderness; the cleft in that chin, by its nearness; and the soft brown eyes, by their very intimacy, caused Chapman's heart to buck, and his stomach suddenly to twist with sickness.

Horror rose up to Chapman's eyes: what did Mr. Lomax *truly* want? What kind of a thing was he *truly* offering? And what had Chapman already given away from his treasure of secrets?

Ah, God!

Chapman drew back from Lomax. He threw himself into the pool, and thrashed the water awkwardly, trying to swim from the corruption behind him. But then he heard the *chomp* of a hard dive into the water; and then Lomax was below him, swimming upward, and then he, Chapman, felt a hand at the band of his swimming trunks, grabbing, tugging. He kicked down with his heel again and again, twice feeling a dull connection of flesh and bone below. He thrashed mightily to the other side, yanked his body up and over the side, then ran to the locker room, where he dressed without drying and dashed away.

On Tuesday, then, when the class began in plainsong to chant the devastation of Mr. Lomax, Chapman astonished himself by yelling along, yelling with a nearly hysterical abandon: "Max beats his wife! MAX BEATS HIS WIFE!"

Mr. Lomax turned from the blackboard.

Everyone fell silent.

Not Chapman.

Once more into the silence, the emotional inertia driving him forward in spite of all, he cried, "MAX BEATS HIS WIFE!"

Lomax looked back directly at him. At Chapman. The brown-eyed gaze might have killed Chapman, except for his own fury and his own righteousness. He stared back.

This time Lomax did not preach. He did not read from the Bible. He uttered only a brief, soft sentence, which caused most boys to frown, not understanding.

Lomax murmured, "Midge. Her name is Margaret."

And then he left the front of the classroom.

But he did not leave the classroom itself. Chapman, in his heart, *commanded* the man just to go away. Go out the door. But he didn't.

Slowly Lomax walked round to the window side of the room, and then back to its corner, where there sat an old upright piano. He was not blushing this time. The skin on his head, instead, was blotchy pale. Chapman could not remove his eyes from watching the man.

Mr. Lomax pulled out the piano stool and sat on it. For one idiot instant, Chapman thought that he might begin to play some sort of music, but he didn't. He bowed his head over the piano keys, and he wept. There was no sound. No sobbing. But Chapman watched the tears drop from his teacher's eyes upon the keys, black and white. Upon the woodwork.

Lomax, it seemed, was completely defeated.

On Wednesday the twenty-first of November, almost all of the students at McLean's Christian Academy went home to celebrate several days of Thanksgiving.

The thing that had happened between himself and Mr. Lomax, Chapman uttered to no one. Certainly not to Alex. Dear Lord, what would *Alex* do with such a story? Not even to his parents. Chapman's parents were oblivious of the life he had to lead at

McLean's. They assumed that all was well. But then, they had assumed the same while he still lived with them, when it wasn't homesickness he felt so much as plain loneliness. His younger sister admired him. Angela would cry every time he left home. These tears seemed to Chapman the closest he came to receiving the hands of Jesus upon his head. They were purest blessing, for his sister's heart was pure, and not even he could sully the purity by doubting or analyzing or explaining the blessing away. She put her arms around him and wept. She blessed him, and he was blessed.

In those days, Chapman was beginning to think that he shouldn't hang out with Haverford so much any more. Neither one of them was much included in the rougher, truer communion of their classmates' activities. Neither one *wanted* to be included, of course; but to hang together and apart from the others seemed, to Chapman, to double their vulnerability to general scorn and mockery.

But Haverford's parents had worked out a deal with Chapman's: if they would take their son on Saturday as far as the Haverford house, he, Chapman, could stay there overnight, to be driven by Haverford's parents back to school on Sunday.

And so it was that Chapman had a second distressing conversation, this time between himself and his classmate, but Mr. Lomax was there as well, for it was *about* him.

Again, out of the blue, Haverford said, "He plays chess, did you know? He's really very good."

They were together in Haverford's bedroom, which was kept so neat that Chapman hardly knew where to sit down. He was, he felt, the only dirt and the only wrinkle in the place. Haverford even had a sit-down dressing table with a mirror, matching comb and brushes, and small bottles of ointments and such.

"Who plays chess?"

"Mr. Lomax. I've been to his house several times. He tends to drink tea. But he'll offer you beer. He's easy."

Chapman wondered how it was that Haverford chose to talk about Lomax now. Did he connect him, Chapman, somehow to the teacher in a special way?

"Why are we talking about Lomax?" Chapman said.

Haverford, sitting on the side of his bed with his legs crossed, glanced up. "I don't know," he said. "It popped into my mind." The boy looked down at this hands, from which could issue the music of heaven. That's what Chapman really wanted to talk about. Music. Not about poetry anymore. At least not his own poetry, nor even that he wrote it. Or cared about writing it.

Suddenly Haverford looked up at Chapman, where he stood leaning against the doorjamb.

"No!" he said. "I know why. The last time I had supper with him, we talked about you."

Cold fear brought Chapman's jaws together with a click. So what *did* people know about things?

"Chapman," Haverford said, "it was his wife. Midge. Her name's Margaret, but Mr. Lomax calls her Midge—and you should get to know her. You would like her. She enjoys cooking for students, she says. Anyway, it was Mrs. Lomax who had really wondered about you. She saw you in chapel. She said that you had an 'arresting' face. That's how she put it. She said that the expression on your face tugged at her heartstrings. 'Deep,' she said. 'That boy is very deep.' But then she said that you were sad about something—"

At these last words Chapman sucked in a swift breath, and then shocked himself by suffering a tremendous urge to burst into tears: *Sad, sad, sad about something.*

Haverford was saying, "She saw an artist in you, and I told her that she was right, you *are* an artist, a writer, and she said that she understood the terrible tenderness of the hearts of artists. Then she said to Mr. Lomax, 'Harold, the next time you have the chance, please invite Mr. Wagenknecht here for a meal. I think,' she said—I remember these words exactly, Chapman, because they sounded so good to me—'I think,' she said, 'that boy needs a mother.'"

And at *that* last word, Chapman lost control. He burst into tears. He wept a howling, lonely sorrow, a hunger too deep to name—and at the same time a whipping, withering shame. For he had without cause sinned against Mr. Lomax. He, Chapman, was wicked. And if he wanted to think only about the things his sin had lost him, why, he had lost a human friend. And, perhaps, a home.

Haverford gazed at Chapman. Softly he said, "Are you all right?"

Chapman shook and shook his head. He went down on his knees and wrapped his arms around his stomach and shook his head.

Haverford said no more. Neither did he come near the impoverished, weeping Chapman. But he didn't leave the room. He offered the quiet consolation of his presence.

And so, when Chapman got his voice back again, Haverford was there to hear him, Chapman, make a promise before God. It was specifically before God that Chapman made this promise, because he wanted it to be real even now, when as yet he could actually *do* nothing about it. And he made it before God because he felt that God had conducted these conversations, starting them "out of the blue," with no request and no prompting from Chapman himself. He, Chapman, was known—and it was not terrible! He was known by Mrs. Lomax. And by Mr. Lomax. And even a little by Haverford. But mostly by God.

Therefore, before God, Chapman said aloud: "On the day after we get back to school, I am going to Mr. Lomax's office. And I am going to tell him that I am sorry. I'm going to tell him how sorry I am, and I am going to beg his forgiveness."

Haverford did not ask, *Sorry for what?*

Haverford was an artist, too. He had more sense than that.

But on Monday the twenty-sixth of November, early in the morning, while students were eating their breakfast in the dining hall, Headmaster Reimer announced with great sorrow that on Thanksgiving day itself Mr. Harold Lomax had passed away. It was a sudden, completely unexpected death.

Alex, who was sitting across from Chapman at the time, poked his right pointer finger into the left side of his neck, then drew a line from ear to ear, as if his finger were a knife.

"Arrrgh!" he guttered deep in his throat. And then, to Chapman's abiding horror, he leaned forward and whispered, "Suicide!"

It was at that moment that Chapman erected his dike against emotion, that he drove all feeling away, because if it came crashing down upon him now, it would drown him, surely.

I was there then, too. I had been with Chapman through every step of the story. I know it well, and very well.

Cicero: *Enim neque assentior his qui nuper coeperunt dissarere haec animos interire simul cum corporibus. . . .*

Chapman Wagenkneckt: "For I do not agree with (approve of?) those who recently began to discuss these things, that the spirits die together with . . . bodies. The bodies. Their bodies . . ."

Even do you translate the words of Cicero. Your attention is altogether on translating, not on understanding. You use the words for "death" and "dying" without actually thinking about death and dying. Because this is possible: that one can do the task only at its surface, never diving deeper to the substance that lies within. The trap that lies within.

Chapman, I think your greatest fear is to admit and identify the one with whom you are truly angry. For that *Whom,* should he take your anger seriously, might just sweep you away from among the living. Or so you think. Or so your young soul *would* think, could you allow it the freedom to think.

Your roommate's radio pours forth a nasal song about love and loss. Country music. It permits you a smaller, nasty anger: Cicero, you argue within yourself, is infinitely more valuable than Tammy Wynette. And Haverford's twitchy fingers are translating Bach and Saint-Saëns, faith and grandeur and glorious joy, better than tinny radios translate pathetic whining.

Cicero: *Atque omnia deleri morte.*

Chapman, laboring hard not to think (but I think I will make him think very soon, in spite of himself): "and that *omnia,* all, all things, everything, is destroyed by . . . *morte,* by death."

Suddenly you stand up, sending your chair backward by the unbending of your knees. Its backrest hits the floor.

Alex makes a breath-noise, surprised by the clamor.

"What?" he says.

You look. He's been lying on his bed, his fingers laced behind his head; but now he's half twisted in your direction.

"What, Chappy?"

You have heard a chord of music from outside, even through the windows, tremendous and vaulting, both lifting and troubling your soul. You march to Alex's annoying radio and snap it off.

"Chappy! Chapman! What are you doing?"

You go to the window and throw it open, and the cold pours in—but there, vibrating in the night, is Haverford's magnificent declaration of faith, and you seek in it some solace, but it seems not to know you, not able to acknowledge you. These grand chords of the organ are like the angels before the throne of God, so full of the glory of the Lord that they cannot attend to anything else, and surely not to a boy who in his fourteenth year is angry, who is spitting bitterness, furious himself at the Lord God.

At the Lord God.

There it is, Chapman. Do you understand? Can you utter the name at the other end of your great rage? Does it terrify you to know it? Will you die, now, admitting that the one with whom you are at war, he is God?

It is the truth.

You blame God for taking Mr. Lomax away before you could apologize and make things right again.

You blame God for withholding the truth about Mr. Lomax all these months, and creating, therefore, the opportunity for you to sin against him, to cut him worse than any other boy in the classroom, or even in your class.

You blame God, Chapman, for the wickedness of your own soul, for you say over and over again: *But I am a good boy. I am good at heart. I never intended to hurt anyone.*

"Arrrgh! Suicide."

Then am I the one who killed him?

Alex flies past you and grabs the window sash and slams it down, crying, "What is the *matter* with you?" But then he turns and sees that you are down on your knees, crying and crying helplessly, and he backs off, his two hands up, palms facing you as if you are a dog with rabies. He looks frightened, his blonde curls trembling. He backs right out of the room, and you don't mind. You don't blame him. You have lost it. There is no pretense now. And whatever the other boys may think of you hereafter, well, you deserve it.

You deserve it: that's what you think, don't you, Chapman?

But whether the window is open or whether it's closed, I am here. I have always been here.

And I am grateful that you aren't trying to keep secrets any more.

Oh, I knew them all along.

But now *you* may know that I have known them and know them even now.

You've never been able to keep secrets from me, whatever powers you thought you had for hiding things. From your parents, perhaps. From the people at McLean's, yes. But not from me. That was a deceit. You were deceiving yourself. You were hiding something, Chapman, from yourself.

But now you know that I know: your tears, therefore, have become an open confession. You sinned. Yes, you sinned. No, Chapman, in all your assessments of Harold Lomax you were not a good boy. It was your fault.

And then you shifted the rage such failure caused in you from yourself to me.

Cry it out, child. Scream it out. Lie down on the ground and wail, till it is all made manifest between us. For I am the one who truly can take your anger and not be changed by it, nor ever withdraw from it or from you. For I am God and not a man, the Holy One in your midst, and I have not come to destroy.

And when you have given tongue to the evil that you have become, and when you have named it for what it is, offering no excuse but truthfulness only, truthfulness as pure as the tears of your sister, then you will know as well my forgiveness. I will take the evil away. And you shall be my child again, and I will be your God.

Even so. Even so.

Now go down. Go out into the night air. Go over to the organ which Haverford is playing. Take a seat in one of the pews, and wait until he notices you. Then ask him if he would be so kind as to play yet one song more before he closes the keys for the night.

Which is the hymn you loved as a child? Into which hymn could you crawl for mother-comfort and for kindness?

Ask him to play that one. And so we'll start all over again.

Putzel, Putzel, I Love You So Much

While I was courting Ruthanne Bohlmann, visiting as often as possible her parental farmhouse in Illinois, I was vouchsafed a gentle, indelible scene.

Though the scene was brief and as common as mother-love everywhere in the world, I've never forgotten it (though my mother-in-law likely had forgotten it by the end of the week). And perhaps *because* it betokens this most common miracle—that mothers can love immediately, with the fullness of their beings, seeking nothing in return to sustain the love that will not cease—I have found in the event and my memory of it a sustenance of my own. I have cherished the vision for more than three decades; and in the end it triggered a genial children's book of love.

In the middle of an autumn afternoon I glanced into the parlor of the farmhouse.

Martin was in the fields, harvesting soybeans. Gertrude had just finished canning tomatoes in the kitchen; had set the hot jars in rows on the table, waiting for the lids to click; was drying her hands on her apron. I had been sitting in the back porch swing, reading a book and watching Martin's combine crawl across the distant fields.

I sneezed. Dust in the air. Or Panda, the dog. I went into a small fit of sneezing, after which I got up and went into the house to blow my nose. As I entered the kitchen, Gertrude was just passing through the doorway into the parlor.

The sweetness and the durability of this memory is that it isn't mine alone. It belongs to Thanne as well, and to her more deeply than to me. What I saw, she saw. Indeed, even today I see it most clearly through her eyes—because the gesture was her mother's, after all. And central to the scene was her sister, Dorothy—whose bed Thanne shared until she left for college, whose round, warm body would curl into Thanne's stomach, comforting her on cold winter's nights.

Gertrude entered the parlor still wiping her hands in her apron, then noticed Dorothy sitting by herself on the floor.

Dorothy has Down's syndrome. In those days she was by the count of her years a teenager. But by intellect and behavior—even by her physical appearance—she was a child. As round and soft as a doughnut hole, frosting-sweet, the slant of her eye seeming ever to smile, short fingers, short stature: if her mother insisted that she eat what she didn't want to eat, Dorothy would break into the sobs of the truly forlorn. But paper delighted her to a giggling glee: paper dolls, paper cuttings from the pictures in *Life* magazine, paper bulletins from church, green paper money—these she hid in wickedly cunning crannies in her bedroom, refusing ever to produce her treasures, however her parents pleaded.

It was, of course, that green paper which caused the greatest fuss. Gertrude supplemented the meager Bohlmann income by baking wedding cakes—this on top of the labor of farming and the administration of a family of fourteen children. Paper money was more precious than coin. And the louder and the fussier she went in search of Dorothy's hiding places, the more worthy became the child's green treasures.

Mother and daughter, willful each, could come to thrilling confrontations. And sometimes the mother won. Sometimes she drew the green paper, all rolled into the thinnest tubes, from the legs of dolls, from chinks in the wall. And then, of course, Dorothy would deliver herself to the sobs of the abandoned.

And so it was that, on an autumn afternoon, I happened to see the bedrock thing upon which the relationship was founded, the thing that never changed, whatever the weather between this mother and her daughter, allowing storms to come and go without a lasting damage.

I saw it fresh. Thanne saw it as another sign of something she'd known all along. This thing: an enduring mother love.

Gertrude, smoothing the apron down her thighs, walked over to Dorothy. The child glanced up, wrinkled her forehead, then put her head down between her knees as if to rain on all the rugs: green paper money, apparently, had vanished again.

But Gertrude knelt and then bent down low, low enough to peer upward into the cloud of the Dorothy-face. Then, suddenly, as if overcome by the sight, Gertrude reached and squeezed her daughter's cheek between the thumb and the fore-knuckle of her right hand. Gently she tugged the little face left and right, left and right, and "*Putzel, Putzel,*" she whispered in a small voice rising toward tears: "Oh, *Putzel,* I love you so much I could eat you up."

As if her daughter were the highest, most royal doll on the crown of the loveliest wedding cake ever baked in Iroquois County, Illinois.

And the Dorothy-face, still staring downward, began to giggle. Silly, silly giggling: like a baby, a tearful giggling. Like a daughter restored. Like a sinner forgiven.

And that's it.

That's the memory we share, Thanne and I. Completely common and as forgettable as bread. Except that people don't forget the staff of life in a world more hungry than whole.

And from such goodness, good stories come, for the artist's job is to notice, to preserve, and to make public these blessings for the sake of the many.

For the children's story is meant as much to embrace the child with health and wholeness as it is to companion the kid through difficulty.

Therefore, my mother-in-law's words became the spirit and the tone of my own tale, written to give voice to any parent's abiding love for the child, *The Bedtime Rhyme*.

With the beginning of that story, I end this story:

> *Are you my strongest?*
> *Are you my smartest?*
> *Are you my baby true?*
>
> *Are you my laughingest,*
> *Loudest and lastingest*
> *Friend? Oh, I love you.*
>
> *I love your eyes*
> *Like fireflies;*
> *I love your ears*
> *Like boutonnieres;*
> *I love your back*
> *Your bones in a sack;*
> *I love your cheeks*
> *And all your teeths,*
> *Your nose and toes and tongue and such—*
>
> *But you say, "Stop! How much? How much?"*
>
> *How much, my honeydew?*
> *How much do I love you?*
> *Lay down your head,*
> *Sweet gingerbread,*
> *And listen: I'll tell you. . . .*

Generations: Adams, Stieglitz, Sendak, and Me

In 1939, Ansel Adams photographed the photographer Alfred Stieglitz standing in one of the corners of his, Stieglitz's, art gallery, An American Place in New York City. Adams was thirty-seven, Stieglitz seventy-five.

The walls and the high ceiling which frame the older man's figure are severely white, barely shadowed at the joins, shorn of interruption, embracing but one dark thing: Stieglitz himself. He holds his glasses loosely at the waist while glancing off to his right. Though the old photographer wears a double-breasted suit, the flaps of the coat pockets reveal slouch, one stuffed altogether in its pocket, the other but half in, one corner poking up like the ear of a fox. The backs of his hands are age-mottled; his eyes are casual, inquisitive, responsive, worn; the bottom edge of his white moustache sheared as ruler-straight as the old man's artistic judgments and principles.

Most folks know that Ansel Adams was a photographer in black and white, in awe-ful communion with nature (*and* with the faces of humans, *and* with their places, too, their habitations, San Francisco, New York).

Fully as many folks should know that Alfred Stieglitz was the first artist self-con-sciously to fight for the recognition of photography as a creative art medium, equal to that of painting. He made this decision as early as the mid-1880's, while studying in Berlin. And his were the first photographs to be hung in reputable museums with the same care and formality accorded the framed painting. Moreover, Stieglitz dedicated his life to supporting and exhibiting the art of artists in America. Photographers. The work, in 1936, of that broad-faced fellow from the west, Ansel Adams.

Adams' photograph of Stieglitz—the entire artistic act, in fact—is an intimate circle between two artists, even as it is a segment of the spiral which winds through countless generations of artists, that unbroken spiral which keeps art organic, changing, living, age to age. The photograph is its own unique and necessary exchange: the tribute of a younger artist for the elder artist who had made a way for him. It is a tribute offered in the medium they shared, a tribute in craft for craft, and by craft to find and define the character of the man honored, to lay bare that which *is* honorable in him: altogether, then, a tribute private and personal, yet meant to be exhibited in public.

Even so is this small volume of mine my tribute to Maurice Sendak, the story-teller in word and vision whom, since 1965, I have seen astonishingly, dangerously present in his own work (the risk of every story-*teller*), whom nevertheless his work conceals by its own sweetness and visceral power.

I cannot take his picture. I cannot draw him. I write to the writer my personal thanksgiving—personal, though my voice is a chorus of the voices of story-purveyors.

⋅§§⋅

In 1978, I published my first novel, *The Book of the Dun Cow,* to some national acclaim. In 1979, Maurice telephoned my house, seeking me but finding my wife instead. He asked her how old I was. Thanne said, "Thirty-five." He responded with two comments. First, he confessed himself glad I was so young, because I would not yet have been driven to "cynicism." Second, he hoped I'd be resilient enough to survive the administrations of publishers with my spirit intact.

I called him back. Access Parnassus? Of course I called him back. We talked at greater length then, and have all down the years corresponded mostly by the patient paper mail. But his manner toward me was established already in that initial chat with Thanne: an elder whose first attentions were for the younger *person* rather than for the techniques of our shared craft; an elder who had already gone the rugged way and was conscious of younger ones following. This is a sign of sanctity, that one who has experienced difficulty does not descend thereafter into a private (perfectly reasonable!) bitterness, but rather imagines the others who may suffer the same experience and who turns, then, in compassion away from himself toward them. Personal suffering is thereby transfigured into sacrifice, and sacrifice into the public good. Even before I knew I needed them, Sendak sent a necessary sustenance, hope and kindness.

And this was at the smack-start of my own publishing career, when I was most malleable and mostly isolated: his word was a thousand times more effective than it might have been later—when, say, the young writer had grown tougher and cynical.

And this was the force of friendship then, that it came from one whom I had admired at a distance, whose work I had studied closely, intensely.

I encountered Sendak when I was a college student in 1965, writing and trying to hone my writing. On impulse I bought two picture books by Maurice Sendak, *Sarah's Room* and *Where the Wild Things Are.* The first was graceful, uncle-funny, Victorian in place and manner, yet intimately contemporary in the sly vengeance Jenny takes on her organized and snobbish older sister Sarah. The first book was wonderfully competent and fun.

But the second book straightway seduced my soul by its deep familiarity and then stunned me by getting the childhood experience (*my* childhood experience) so right as to finish things unfinished before!

Familiar: Max, the boy who is banished by his mother to his room with nothing to eat; Max, who by the power of an angry imagination turns his bedroom into a forest and thereafter finds the island where the "Wild Things" are, into whose eyes Max stares so fiercely that they back down!—this Max both revived and put flesh to my own lost memories. I had been weaned on the Grimm brothers and Hans Christian Andersen; the second a melancholy and sometimes uncompromising story-teller, the first lacking any story-teller at all. Here was a tale of fright and fight *with* a teller who knew my secrets, who was willing to confront the truth, and who danced like the piper in front of me, assuring me of safe endings. Sendak accomplished "presence" by the tone of his voice and the mood of his line. And I, the child and the writer, followed to the finish. For once I had fantasized myself out of a difficult house. I had, without ever admitting it, been angry, been furious at authorities stronger and bigger than I. I had sought power in my most powerless state. . . .

Familiar: the Germanic tales collected by the Grimm brothers, the northern European stories of Andersen had come to me from timeless islands far away, at mystic removes from my small self. *Where the Wild Things Are,* on the other hand, was familiar in that it had been born right beside me, in this world, this culture, this time, this language, the stuff of my present context. It was mine. No citizen of my country had ever so rightly acknowledged and so rightly construed my private striving, making it a shared thing, calling me out of myself. Well, of course: Sendak has said over and over that the fantasy story which works well had been and "must be rooted in living fact." He and all his readers shared living facts both timeless and timely.

Following the discovery of this one picture book (by the college student who as an innocent received its story and its silly/serious portraits of the wild things themselves) I—the writer, now—paid close attention to Sendak's work, both the art and the effect of the art. I modeled my writing upon his sensibilities, the *artist's* relationship to his work, the artist's relationship to the readers receiving the work, characteristics, as I've said, which are apparent even in his color, his line, his language. The figures of the wild things, for example, are in fact an artist's communication of terrible, wary-ful, shark-toothy, animal-horned and animal-clawed beasts, rendered with *tenderness,* for they are also reminiscent by hair and expression and grouping of mothers and fathers and siblings. This is the relationship I have since conned and sought to establish with my own readers.

Too, Sendak had opened the path for—and had himself proven the value of—storifying even for children the difficult truths of evil and suffering in order to assure them of goodness, of courage, and of rising up again. His work set my work free of a certain cultural lisp: the "pastel-ing," the candy-ing of childhood experience, that adult condescension which avoids conflicts at the deeper levels of right and wrong, anger and fierce love, fears and triumphs, life and death.

This is the artist who called me at home in 1979, the one whom I had known and studied and admired for years. How could his call not have come with a transcending force? Sendak "Somewhere"; Sendak "Successful"; Sendak of another sphere; Sendak *Parnassian* was suddenly Sendak with slouch in his voice, one flap of his jacket stuffed into the pocket, the other one dog-eared. His simple kindness transfigured not only the man for me, but also the glory of his art. I mean "glory" as does the Hebrew Scripture with the word *kabod:* his weightiness, his earned and innate authority. This was no longer the distant thing toward which I struggled on my own; it was suddenly a gift, a personal exchange—which made it for me a possibility. And personal possibility is hope. And hope does not disappoint us.

Though an artist might guess the influence of his art upon another's, I doubt that Sendak knew the effect his *kindness* had upon me and my art—or that he knows now the personal blessing of our correspondences since.

The commandment to "honor" our elders is a commandment to acknowledge and to return unto them the *kabod* by which they had affected our lives. The Hebrew word for "honor" is a cognate of the word *kabod:* weight for weight we offer the elder: glory for glory. It is the commandment with a promise: that as long as the younger honors the elder; as long as honor spirals generation to generation through many generations, even so long shall a people live in the land the Lord God has given them. Has given us: the land Parnassian. The abode of poets.

Honoring the elder is not the stoking of some private pride. Like suffering turned into sacrifice for the public good, so tribute brings a broad benefaction to a whole people.

It is time, then, to speak clearly of the effect that Maurice Sendak has had upon me and many. . . .

In November 1936, the year of the photograph, Alfred Stieglitz mounted a show of Ansel Adams' work. On November 29 of that year, Adams wrote to Stieglitz a letter:

> My work has become new and exciting to me as never before. The praise you give never nourishes conceit—it reveals too much of the future for that. . . . I can see only one thing to do—make the photography as clean, as decisive, and as honest as possible. It will find its own level.

Sendak's character and his response, likewise, to *The Book of the Dun Cow* and later to other children's stories such as *Thistle,* has had the very same effect upon me: a nearly moral call to the rightness of my writing, that it be clean, decisive, *honest.*

In 1985, some forty years after Stieglitz's death, Adams defined the quality of the older man's influence upon him: "I would say that he revealed me to myself. Paul Strand's work showed me the potential of photography as an art form; Stieglitz gave me the confidence that I could express myself through that art form. . . . [H]e possessed the very rare quality of spiritual independence."

Though I have never met Maurice Sendak face to face, this is precisely the legacy an elder artist can bequeath his junior by kindness and by the personalization of his public work, something more than technique, something of a far greater advantage: confidence, freedom, a living model rather than the fixed blueprint for one's art. A path. A vulnerability and *nevertheless* a surviving spirit.

"How old is he?"

"Thirty-five."

"Good! He hasn't yet been driven to cynicism. . . ."

Maurice, in February this year, 2001, I turned fifty-seven. In June you turned seventy-three.

Please accept this volume as evidence of a reflected glory and as a token of my own gratitude. Your person and your art have breathed upon the craft herein, the thought, the writer. And I make my thanksgivings public because a great portion *of* the public—writers and artists in particular—have matured under your tender, tumultuous skies. I speak for a people.

For this is how the thing must always go: from person to persons, from older to younger, from mentor to students. Art is never an isolated thing. It is generational. It is the bequest of one to others, a legacy to be fought with, to be admired, to be copied or developed or transfigured—to be received.

Our struggles may be personal and private, Maurice, yours and mine. But the consequences thereof, uttered in art, create a public intimacy after all, and a common dwelling place. Even alone, we are not alone.

Walter Wangerin, Jr.
June 12, 2001

Other Books by Walter Wangerin, Jr.

Fiction

The Book of the Dun Cow, Harper & Row, 1978

The Crying for a Vision, Simon & Schuster, 1994*

The Book of God: The Bible as a Novel, Lion UK and Zondervan, 1996.

The Book of Sorrows, Zondervan, 1996

Paul: A Novel, Lion UK and Zondervan, 2000

Children's Books

Elisabeth and the Water-Troll, HarperCollins Children's Books, 1991*

Branta and the Golden Stone, Simon & Schuster, 1993*

Potter, Augsburg Fortress, 1994

Thistle, Augsburg Fortress, 1995

Probity Jones and the Fear Not Angel, Augsburg Fortress, 1996

The Book of God for Children, Zondervan, 1996*

In the Beginning, There Was No Sky, Augsburg Fortress, 1997

Mary's First Christmas, Zondervan, 1998

The Bedtime Rhyme, Augsburg Fortress, 1998

Water, Come Down!, Augsburg Fortress, 1999

Peter's First Easter, Zondervan, 2000

Collections of Short Stories and Essays
Ragman and Other Cries of Faith, Harper & Row, 1984

Miz Lil and the Chronicles of Grace, Harper & Row, 1988*

The Manger Is Empty, Harper & Row, 1989*

Little Lamb, Who Made Thee?, Zondervan, 1993

In the Days of the Angels, WaterBrook Press, 2000

Practical Theology
As for Me and My House: Crafting a Marriage to Last, Thomas Nelson, 1987

Mourning into Dancing, Zondervan, 1992

The Orphean Passages: The Drama of Faith, Zondervan, 1996

Whole Prayer, Zondervan, 1998

Prayerbook for Husbands and Wives, Augsburg Fortress, 2000

Devotional
Reliving the Passion, Zondervan, 1992

Preparing for Jesus, Zondervan, 1999

* *Denotes out-of-print title*

RELATED TITLES FROM AUGSBURG

The Classic Treasury of Children's Prayers
compiled by Susan Cuthbert, illustrated by Alison Jay
224 pages, 0-8066-4070-7

With more than 200 selections of favorite prayers from the Bible and beloved poets, plus rhyming prayers for younger children, this book is the ideal point at which children can begin building their faith.

Twilight Verses, Moonlight Rhymes
compiled by Mary Joslin, illustrated by Liz Pichon
60 pages, 0-8066-3885-0

A wonderful book of rhymes, both traditional and modern, to learn and say together with your child.

Tumbler by Liz Filleul, illustrated by Susan Field
32 pages, 0-8066-4268-8

A charming legend of Tristan the Tumbler, beautifully retold, this story offers thoughtful insights about the worth and uniqueness of each person.

Best-Loved Parables by Lois Rock, illustrated by Gail Newey
48 pages, 0-8066-3951-2

A book of stories retold for children in a lively and engaging style, while retaining the resonances of the Gospel accounts in the Bible that have preserved them as part of the world's heritage for nearly two thousand years.

Available wherever books are sold.
To order these books directly, contact:
1-800-328-4648 • www.augsburgfortress.org
Augsburg Fortress, Publishers
P.O. Box 1209, Minneapolis, MN 55440-1209